The Janus Employabi

Job Interview Guide

MW01202019

Arnold Livingstone

Consultant
Martin Kimeldorf
Job Search Education Consultant
Tumwater, Washington

GLOBE FEARON
EDUCATIONAL PUBLISHER
A Division of Simon & Schuster

The Janus Employability Skills Program
Job Planner
Job Application File
Job Interview Guide
Job Interview PracticePak
Get Hired!
Don't Get Fired!
Payday! Managing Your Paycheck
Teacher's Guide and Resource:
Employability Skills Program

Designers: Michael Rogondino, E. Carol Gee,
 and C. Buck Reynolds, Pat Smythe
Executive Editor: Joan Wolfgang, Joan Carrafiello
Editor: Renee E. Beach
Production Service: Jeanine Ardourel & Associates
Production Manager: E. Carol Gee
Production Director: Penny Gibson
Senior Production Editor: Linda Greenberg
Desktop Supervisor: José López
Production Editor: Walt Niedner
Manufacturing Administrator: Elizabeth L. Tong
Composition Administrator: Arlene Hardwick
Marketing: Marge Curson

Compositor: Letter Perfect Typography
Printer: Bindco

Printed in the United States of America
 4 5 6 7 8 9 10 99

ISBN: 0-835-91413-5

GLOBE FEARON
EDUCATIONAL PUBLISHER
A Division of Simon & Schuster

Acknowledgments: We would like to thank the
following individuals and organizations for their
time and generosity in assisting with the
photography for this book: Lisa Mitchell, FPG,
New York City; Public Relations Dept., Hewlett-
Packard, Palo Alto; Sabatino and Robert Scialanga,
Mission Market Fish & Poultry, San Francisco;
Thomas McGarry, Mt. Eden Hospital, Castro
Valley; Joyce Icasiano, Jack-in-the-Box, Hayward;
Cindy Delumen, Grade-Way Construction Co.,
Fremont; Ellen Bunning, Jeroboam, San Francisco;
K-Mart, Hayward; Petite Sophisticates, Hayward;
California Couriers, Hayward; Dick Hunter and
The Work Control Center at U.C. Hayward;
Dr. Phyllis Kaplan; Student Employment Offices at
Chabot College, Hayward and Ohlone College,
Fremont

Photo Credits
Jerry J. Puff
 pages: 8, 13, 14, 17b, 18, 19, 29, 30, 31, 33b, 34,
 35, 41b, 42, 43, 49a, 53, 54, 55, 57a, 65b, 66, 67,
 73b, 74, 75, 78b, 79
Stone & Stecatti
 pages: 1, 3, 5, 6, 7, 9, 10, 11, 12, 21, 22, 23, 25b,
 26, 27, 37, 38, 39, 41a, 45, 46, 47, 49b, 50, 51, 57b,
 58, 59, 61, 62, 63, 69, 70, 71, 73a, 77a, 78a,
Michael Price/FPG page 17a
Susan Ylvisaker/Uniphoto page 25a
Photo Courtesy of Hewlett-Packard Co. page 33a
Ellen Bunning/Jeroboam page 65a
Elizabeth L. Tong page 77a
Photo Shoot coordinator: Michele Serbin
© David Soo page 13
Bob Daemmrich/Stock Boston page 14
Ellis Herwig/Stock Boston page 17
Jenifer Hixson, page 21
Dean Anderson/Stock Boston page 37

Contents

Introduction

When you apply for a job, you will have to talk to someone who does the hiring. That person is usually called a *job interviewer*. The talk you have with the interviewer is called a *job interview*. This book will help you get ready to meet and talk with real job interviewers.

An interviewer tries to find out if you are the right person for a job opening he or she wants to fill. At the same time, you can try to find out if the job and the place of employment are what you want.

Getting a good job usually depends on two things:
- filling out a job application well, and
- doing well in a job interview.

If you make a good impression in the application and interview, you may get the job. You may get it even if you don't meet all the qualifications the interviewer is looking for. If you make a bad impression, no matter how qualified you are, you will lose your chance for getting the job.

This book will be your guide on how to make a good impression during a job interview. First, it will explain what takes place during a job interview. Then it will give you some helpful guidelines on what to do before, during, and after an interview.

Then, you will read 15 different job interviews. You will read exactly what the applicants and the interviewers say. You will get a chance to decide for yourself what the job applicants did well or not so well, and how they can do better next time.

Finally, you will get a chance to practice being a job applicant, so you can try out what you have learned.

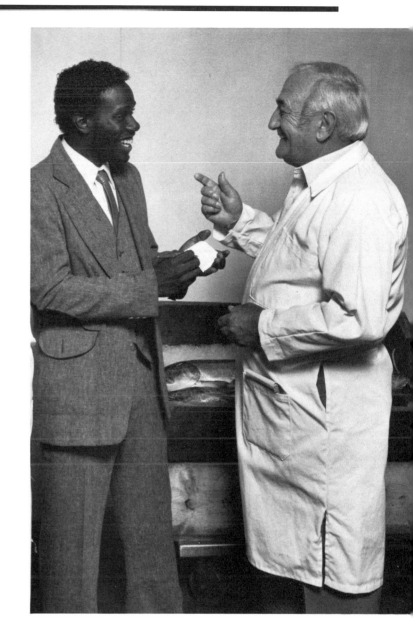

What to Expect at an Interview ____

Large companies have special interviewers.

Two people talking—one asking questions and the other answering—that is an interview. In the case of a job interview, most of the questions are asked by the interviewer. And most of the answers are given by the job applicant.

Of course, an interview is not all one-sided. The applicant also gets to ask questions. The applicant can ask for information about the job and the place of employment.

As an applicant, you need to try to please the interviewer by the way you look, act, and talk. You need to listen and answer carefully. You need to be relaxed, honest, and businesslike. You must make the interviewer believe that you are the best possible person for the job.

Where and Who

A job interview may take place in a personnel department of a large company, an office of a small business, or at a job site.

The person who interviews you may be a personnel interviewer. Or, he or she might be the employer who owns the business. This is often true when the company is very small or where the employer is a doctor, dentist, or similar professional person. You may also be interviewed by a manager of a small business.

The word *employer* can also mean the company itself, not just the owner of the company. In most large companies, you will first be interviewed in the personnel department. If that interview goes very well, your second interviewer might be the person for whom you would be working.

6

When you don't make a good impression on an interviewer, you don't get hired. If you make a good impression, you may get hired or you may qualify for another interview. This second interview is only for applicants who have a good chance to get the job.

Most employers are very careful about filling a job opening. They usually don't hire until they have interviewed several applicants. They want the best person they can find. So be prepared. Follow the guidelines on pages 8–15.

Summary

Fill in the word that best completes each sentence. Then read the summary to review what you have learned.

employer   **office**
impression   **talk**
interviewer

1. In a job interview, most of the questions are asked by the job _____.

2. You have to try and please the interviewer by the way you look, act, and _____.

3. The interview may take place in an _____ or on the job site.

4. The person who interviews you may be a personnel interviewer, the person for whom you would be working, or the _____.

5. No matter who does the interviewing, it is important that you make a good _____.

In a very small business, you may be interviewed by the employer who owns the business.

Guidelines for Job Applicants _____

On pages 8–15, you will find out what to do before, during, and after a job interview.

Practice, if you think you may have to show what you can do.

A. Preparing Yourself

1. Prepare a paper with information you will need to complete a job application. Include your Social Security and driver's license numbers. List the names, addresses, and phone numbers of the following:
   - the schools you have attended,
   - your previous employers, and
   - three people who know you besides relatives and former employers.

   Bring the sheet with you anytime you have to fill out a job application.*
2. Decide how much money you need to live on. Remember, what you earn is not what you take home. Employers must take deductions for taxes and other things. Ask at the interview what the take-home part of the salary is. Then you will know if the salary being offered will be enough to meet your needs.
3. Think about your other needs.
   - Do you want to work in a place where there are lots of people your age?
   - Must you have your nights and weekends free?
   - Would you mind working downtown? in a factory district? in a quiet place? and so on.
   - How would you get to and from a job? Would you mind commuting? Could you afford to commute?
4. Find out all you can about the job you are applying for and about the employer. This will help you to prepare questions to ask at the interview. It will also show the interviewer that you really are interested in the job. You might want to find out:
   - what the employer makes or does,
   - the kinds of entry level or beginning jobs the company has,
   - how the chances are for moving up on the job,
   - how many employees the company has,
   - how long the company has been in business, and
   - how well the business is doing.

   You can try to get this information by talking to people who already work there. A local business library or the Chamber of Commerce may have information about some employers. Some large companies give out information about themselves.

*Teachers: See the duplicatable Job Application Information Sheet on pages 5 and 6 of the Teacher's Manual accompanying this book.

5. Prepare a list of questions to ask the interviewer. The questions might be about salary, benefits, working conditions or other things about the job that concern you. If these things do not come up during the interview, ask about them before you leave.

6. Prepare for any tests you may have to take.
   - Practice typing if you are going to interview for a typing job. Practice keyboarding if you are going for a word processing or data entry job.
   - Go over your arithmetic if you are planning to interview for a job that requires handling money or using figures and measurements.
   - Get in shape or take any training you may need if you have to pass a test of physical strength or ability.
   - Remember, you will do better in any test if you stay calm.

7. Be sure that you can get to the interview on time, and that you have a way to get there.
   - Get a schedule, if you are going to use public transportation. Plan the way you will go and the time you will need to allow for the trip.
   - If you are driving, make sure you know the way. If someone else will be doing the driving, make sure they know the way and can get you there on time.
   - Make a practice trip if you can.
   - If you have an appointment to see a special interviewer, call before you leave. Make sure the person you are supposed to see is in and can see you as planned.

Summary

Fill in the word that best completes each sentence. Then read the summary to review what you have learned.

application	money
employer	practice
interview	questions

1. Prepare a paper with information you will need to complete a job

   _____.

2. Decide how much _____ you need to live on.

3. Find out all you can about the

   _____.

4. Prepare a list of _____ to ask the interviewer.

5. Prepare and _____ for any tests you may have to take.

6. Be sure you can get to the _____ on time.

If you have an appointment to see someone special, call before you leave. Make sure the person is in.

Guidelines for Job Applicants

B. Grooming, Clothing, and Things to Bring

1. Good grooming shows an interviewer that you care about yourself and others.
   - Bathe or shower, wash your hair, and brush your teeth.
   - Men should shave and not use any strong after-shave lotions.
   - Women should not use too much perfume or makeup.
   - Get a good night's sleep the night before so you look fresh and rested.
2. Dress in a style that fits the job:
   - Dress simply. Don't wear party-style clothes or a lot of jewelry.
   - For office jobs and most public-contact jobs, dress in a business style. Men should wear clean shirts and slacks and perhaps a jacket and tie. Women should wear dresses or skirts and blouses.
   - For jobs that call for physical work, and where you might be asked to start work right away, wear work clothes to the interview.

Clean, neat clothing and good grooming make a good impression on interviewers.

   - Whatever you wear, make sure your clothes are clean and neat.
3. Be sure to bring these things with you:
   - Your own pen. You may need it to fill out forms.
   - Any special documents you may need to show the interviewer—such as licenses, diplomas, certificates, and work permits.
   - The list of questions you prepared to ask the interviewer.
   - The name and title of the person you are to see or the name of the department you are to go to.
   - The information you prepared to help you fill out job applications.

Summary

Fill in the word that best completes each sentence. Then read the summary to review what you have learned.

information	style
jewelry	title
rested	

1. Look clean, neat, and _____.
2. Dress in a _____ that fits the job.
3. Don't wear too much perfume, after-shave lotion, or _____.
4. Bring along a pen and any documents and _____ you may need.
5. Remember to bring the name and _____ of the person you are to see.

C. Arriving at the Interview

1. Be on time for the interview. Get there five or ten minutes ahead of time. Give yourself a chance to relax and get yourself organized.

2. Don't get there *too* early. Waiting too long might make you more nervous. If you are early, go to the restroom and freshen up.

3. If you have been smoking or eating before the interview, chew a breath freshener before going in.

4. If a friend has come with you, the friend should wait outside.

5. Use good manners from the moment you walk in the door. Be polite to the receptionist who greets you and to other employees you meet. The interviewer may ask them what they think of you after you leave.

6. Take a close look around you. Ask yourself these questions:
   • Do the employees look and act as if they enjoy their work? Or do they look and act gloomy or unhappy?
   • Is this the kind of place I would like to work in?

   If you get hired, you might be working in another part of the building, or in another building. Later, if the interview goes well, ask if you can see where you would be working. Ask yourself how well you would like working there.

7. If you have to take a test or fill out an application, make sure you understand what you are to do. Politely ask the person in charge to explain anything you don't understand.

Be polite to everyone from the time you enter until the time you leave.

Summary

Fill in the word that best completes each sentence. Then read the summary to review what you have learned.

charge	**outside**
employees	**polite**
five	

1. Get to the interview about _____ minutes early.

2. Anyone who has come with you should wait _____.

3. Be _____ to everyone.

4. Try to see if the _____ like their jobs by watching how they look and act.

5. If you have any questions about an application or test, ask the person in _____.

11

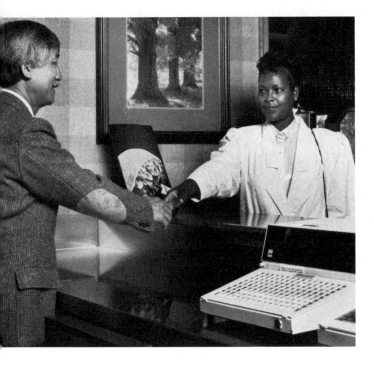

A woman should offer her hand first if the interviewer is a man.

D. Making a Good Impression

1. When you meet the interviewer, show a pleasing personality. Smile and be friendly, but not *too* friendly. Getting too friendly is not businesslike and makes a bad impression. Never call the interviewer by his or her first name, even if the interviewer uses your first name.

2. Maintain good posture and body control. Walk and stand straight, with your head up. Don't twist your hands, shift your weight, or move around the room. Wait until the interviewer asks you to sit down before you take a seat. When you do sit down, sit with your back straight and both feet on the floor. Keep your legs together and sit still during the interview.

3. Show good manners. A man should not put out his hand to shake until the interviewer offers his or hers. If you are a woman, you should offer to shake hands if the interviewer is a man. When you shake hands, be firm. But don't grip or shake the interviewer's hand too hard or too long. Be polite throughout the interview.

4. Make good eye contact. Look straight at the interviewer as much as possible.

5. Don't interrupt the interviewer. When it is time for you to speak, speak in a clear strong voice. Use your best English. Avoid slang and street language. How you speak is usually more important for office or public contact work than for other jobs. But speaking well always makes a good impression on an interviewer.

6 Don't chew gum or smoke.

7. Have a positive attitude. Talk about your good points. Let the interviewer know why you are qualified for the job. Remember, if you don't think well of yourself you can't expect others to think well of you. But beware of talking *too* much about yourself, or of bragging about the things you have done. Being confident makes a good impression but showing off does not.

8. Some interviewers may make a bad impression on you. If an interviewer is rude, try to remain calm and polite. Your next interview will be better.

Summary

Fill in the word that best completes each sentence. Then read the summary to review what you have learned.

attitude	**interrupt**
calm	**interviewer**
friendly	**smoke**
handshake	**straight**
impression	

1. When you meet the interviewer, smile and be _____.

2. Men, wait for the interviewer to put out his or her hand for a _____ before you offer yours.

3. Women, offer to shake hands if the _____ is a man.

4. Don't _____ the interviewer.

5. Speaking well always makes a good _____ on an interviewer.

6. Sit up straight and look _____ at the interviewer.

7. Don't _____ or chew gum.

8. Show you have a good _____ about yourself by talking about your good points.

9. If an interviewer is rude to you, try to remain _____ and polite.

Sit straight, listen carefully, and look at the interviewer most of the time.

E. Listening and Answering

1. Listen carefully to the interviewer. Remember not to interrupt. Answer questions as fully as you can. Give more than a one-word answer when necessary, but don't tell more than the question asked for.

2. The government does not allow job interviewers to ask questions about things that have nothing to do with your qualifications for the job. If you hear such a question, quietly ask the interviewer: "What does that question have to do with my ability to do the job?" Listen to the reply. Then, if you think the question is unfair, you may politely refuse to answer it.

Being reasonable during the interview is a good sign that you can get along with people.

3. Most job applications have questions about convictions for crimes and about health problems. If you have ever been convicted or if you do have a health problem, it is best to write "to be explained" on the application. Then, at the start of the interview, ask if you may explain.

4. Don't try to control the interview. Except for explaining about important questions you did not answer on your application, let the interviewer direct the interview. Wait until he or she asks you if you have any questions. Then you can bring up anything that has not been covered.

5. It is best not to discuss personal, family, or money problems. They are not going to make the interviewer feel sorry for you and give you a job. In fact, telling about your problems usually gives the interviewer a bad impression of you.

6. Show the interviewer that you are reasonable and willing to learn. If you have no experience, say you are willing to start at an entry or beginning level and get on-the-job training. Learn about the job that is being offered and decide if it meets your needs. Being reasonable during the interview shows that you want to get along with people. Being willing to learn shows that you have the motivation or interest to do a good job.

Summary

Fill in the word that best completes each sentence. Then read the summary to review what you have learned.

direct	**money**
explain	**reasonable**
fully	**refuse**

1. Listen carefully to the interviewer and answer questions as _____ as you can.

2. If a question does not seem to have anything to do with how well you can do the job, you may politely _____ to answer it.

3. If you didn't answer some questions on your application, _____ the answers to the interviewer.

4. Let the interviewer _____ the interview.

5. Don't bring up personal, family, or _____ problems.

6. Show the interviewer that you are _____.

F. Closing the Interview

Remember that the last impression may be as important as the first impression. So close the interview well. Usually the interviewer will signal when it is time for you to go. He or she may stand up and thank you for coming in.

1. If you are sure you don't want the job, let the interviewer know it before you leave. You can say why, too, if you like. But if you are interested in the job, tell the interviewer.

2. If you are qualified for the job, the interviewer may tell you. But chances are there are other applicants to be interviewed. And perhaps someone will be checking on the answers and information you wrote on your job application. So don't expect to learn if you have the job for several days, or even weeks.

3. Thank the interviewer for seeing you. Shake hands using the same guidelines you did at the beginning of the interview. (See page 12.) Then leave, walking out as straight as you entered.

4. If you are interested in the job, write or call the interviewer. Keep the call or letter short and simple. Just thank the interviewer again for giving you an interview. Say once again that you are interested in the job.

Summary

Fill in the word that best completes each sentence. Then read the summary to review what you have learned.

interested	seeing
letter	weeks

1. Let the interviewer know whether or not you are _____ in the job.

2. Be prepared to wait several days or even _____ before you find out if you have the job.

3. Thank the interviewer for _____ you.

4. If you want the job, call or write a short _____.

10 STEPS TO A SUCCESSFUL JOB INTERVIEW

1. Decide in advance what you will need at the interview and be sure to bring it.
2. Look clean, fresh, and neat.
3. Be on time.
4. Be honest, friendly, and businesslike.
5. Do not chew gum or smoke.
6. Look at the interviewer and listen carefully.
7. Try to answer questions fully and in a clear, strong voice.
8. Let the interviewer know why you would make a good employee.
9. Ask questions about important things the interviewer did not talk about.
10. Thank the interviewer for seeing you.

Applicants in Action

How to Read Each Interview Section

1. Read the first page. Learn all you can about the job and the applicant.
2. Read the "Directions" on the second page very carefully.
3. Follow the directions as you read the interview, silently or aloud.
4. Do the "What Do You Think?" exercises on the fourth page.

How to Rate Each Applicant

An interviewer often makes a decision about an applicant based on his or her first impression of the applicant. After you read each interview, you will decide what kind of first impression the applicant made on you. You will use a rating form like the one shown at the right to help you make that decision. Here is how to use the form:

1. Write in the score you think the applicant deserves for each item on the "First Impressions" form. Be ready to tell why you chose each score.
2. Add up the scores.
3. Check the rating that shows the number range that includes your total score. That rating is your overall first impression.

Ask yourself these questions as you rate each applicant:

Grooming Does the applicant look clean and neat?

Clothing Are the applicant's clothes appropriate for the interview?

Posture/Body Control Does the applicant stand and sit straight, without slouching? Does he or she seem to sit or stand still?

Eye Contact Does the applicant look straight at the interviewer during most of the interview?

First Impressions

Scoring Excellent 15   Fair 5
Good 10   Poor 0

Item	Score
Grooming	
Clothing	
Posture/Body Control	
Eye Contact	
Manners	
Language	
Personality	
Total	

Rating ☐ Excellent 91–105   ☐ Fair . . 31–65
☐ Good 66–90   ☐ Poor . . 0–30

Manners Is the applicant polite? Does he or she follow the guidelines about handshakes?

Language Is the applicant's way of speaking appropriate for the interview?

Personality Is the applicant cheerful and friendly, without being *too* friendly?

Cannery Worker

The Job

A cannery worker may:
- place food products on conveyors
- sort products by size, color, or quality
- feed processing machines
- trim, peel, or slice products
- clean glass containers
- feed containers to conveyor
- fill containers
- count filled containers
- inspect and weigh filled containers
- put containers in boxes
- move boxes to storage or shipping areas

The Applicant

Fred Walker lives in Middletown, a small city in the farming area of Caspar Valley. He has finished high school and is looking for a job.

Fred has experience working on a farm. His father used to own one. But there are few farm jobs these days. Machines do most of the work. For the last two summers, Fred worked for a packing company, boxing vegetables in the fields.

Fred has decided to get a job where he can put his experience to some use. He is trying to find work with one of the seven large food processing companies in the valley. The companies can fruits and vegetables and pack frozen vegetables.

Fred has called the personnel departments of all seven companies to ask about job openings. Only one of the companies—Delicacy Foods—is hiring workers. Fred was told to come in for an interview with the plant foreman, Larry Tonaka. Right now, Fred is meeting with Mr. Tonaka.

Fred and Mr. Tonaka

Directions

- Use the photos to rate Fred's grooming, clothing, posture, body control, and eye contact.
- As you read the interview, note Fred's manners, language, personality, preparation, attitude, motivation, and qualifications. Also note the way he listens, the answers he gives, and the questions he asks.
- <u>Underline</u> any of Fred's statements that may help him get the job. (Circle) any of Fred's statements that may hurt his chances. | Box | any statements that may not be harmful but could be improved.

SECRETARY: Mr. Tonaka, this is Fred Walker. (She leaves.)

FRED: How do you do, sir. (He puts out his hand for a handshake.)

MR. TONAKA: Hello, Fred. (He shakes Fred's hand.) Just give me a minute to go over your application. (He studies the form.) I see that you worked for Brightday Packers. What did you do for them?

FRED: I was with the field crew. We boxed vegetables. Last summer I was assistant crew chief.

MR. TONAKA: Did you miss many days of work with Brightday?

FRED: No, sir. Last summer I missed only three days. That was when I got my hand caught in the box banding machine.

MR. TONAKA: You caught your hand? How is it now?

FRED: Oh, it's fine now, Mr. Tonaka. See? It's just the little finger of my left hand. I can't move it as much. But it's no problem.

MR. TONAKA: Tell me about yourself, Fred.

FRED: Well, there's not much to tell. I graduated from Middletown High last week. I live with my father and my brothers and sister. Dad used to have a farm out by Hogan's creek. He sold it to the Caspar Valley Land Company when I was 15. Now he has a dry cleaning store. But there's not enough work for all of us, so—

MR. TONAKA: Is there any special reason you want to work for Delicacy Food Products?

FRED: Well, I heard this is a good place
to work. I think jobs with the canneries
are the best-paying jobs in the valley.
I guess it's just that I want to get a good
job. I don't know much about the work
though. I—

MR. TONAKA: Come along with me, Fred.
I'll show you what the production line
looks like. (He takes Fred on a tour.)
These people are sorting. Ever see a
cannery production line before?

FRED: No, sir.

MR. TONAKA: Think you would like to
do this kind of work?

FRED: Yes, sir. I think so.

MR. TONAKA: You know, during harvests
we often have to work overtime. Would
you be willing to work nights, maybe
weekends?

FRED: Yes, sir. I know how important it is
with some crops to get them processed
right away. We worked into the night
many times when I was with Brightday.
And I have worked on farms all my life.

MR. TONAKA: A lot of the work here
involves moving and lifting heavy things.
Do you think you could handle that?

FRED: Sure I could, Mr. Tonaka! I learned
how to handle heavy loads when I
worked for Brightday.

MR. TONAKA: Well all right, Fred. I think
we are going to hire another person next
week. The job pays six dollars ($6.00) an
hour. It's on the production line. There is
a 40-hour week, with time-and-a-half for
overtime....I'll have to check out your
application. I'll let you know one way
or the other by the end of the week.
How is that?

FRED: That sounds fine to me. Thank you,
sir. Good-bye.

What Do You Think?

Rating the Applicant

A. Use the form below to show the kind of first impression Fred made on you. See page 16 for directions.

```
┌─────────────────────────────────────────────┐
│              First Impressions                │
│ Scoring  Excellent.......15  Fair........5    │
│          Good .........10   Poor........0     │
```

Item	Score
Grooming	
Clothing	
Posture/Body Control	
Eye Contact	
Manners	
Language	
Personality	
Total	

Rating ☐ Excellent 91–105 ☐ Fair . .31–65
☐ Good . . . .66–90 ☐ Poor . .0–30

B. Rate Fred on each item below. Be ready to explain your rating.
1. **Preparation** (Was Fred well prepared for the interview?)
☐ Excellent ☐ Fair
☐ Good ☐ Poor
2. **Attitude** (Does Fred seem mostly positive or negative about himself, his previous jobs, and the new job?)
☐ Excellent ☐ Fair
☐ Good ☐ Poor
3. **Motivation** (Does Fred seem to really want the job?)
☐ Excellent ☐ Fair
☐ Good ☐ Poor
4. **Qualifications** (Does Fred seem to have the abilities and experience to do well on the job?)
☐ Excellent ☐ Fair
☐ Good ☐ Poor

Rating, *Continued*

5. **Listening/Answering/Asking** (Does Fred listen carefully, answer all questions fully, and ask important questions?)
☐ Excellent ☐ Fair
☐ Good ☐ Poor

Close-up on the Interview

A. Write **T** if the statement is true. Write **F** if it is false. Be ready to explain your answer.
___ 1. Fred should not have offered to shake hands unless Mr. Tonaka did.
___ 2. Fred should have worn a tie and sports jacket to the interview.
___ 3. Fred should have found out more about cannery jobs before he went for the interview.
___ 4. Fred should have talked about his school and work experience, not about his family.

B. If you were Mr. Tonaka, would you hire Fred?
☐ Yes ☐ No Why or why not?

_____
_____
_____
_____
_____

C. If you could talk to Fred, what advice would you give him?

_____
_____
_____
_____
_____

Bonus

Suppose an interviewer asked you to tell about yourself. What would you say?

Clerk-typist

The Job

A clerk-typist may:
- type letters, statements, bills, and other items
- read, sort, and file forms and records
- address and stuff envelopes
- answer telephones, give messages, and run errands
- open, stamp, sort, and deliver office mail
- stamp forms
- run office copying machines

The Applicant

Catherine Morales moved to River City two weeks ago. She is looking for work through the Perfect Match Employment Agency. She has already been sent out on a few job interviews. But so far she has not been hired.

Today, Catherine has an appointment for an interview at the Ace Plumbing Supplies Company. The woman at the agency said that the company was looking for someone to replace a clerk-typist who was leaving soon.

Catherine was disappointed to discover that the Ace Plumbing Supplies Company is in an old, run-down part of town. It is also a long way by bus from where she is living.

Catherine is nervous. But she is trying not to show it. She is hoping that she does not have to take a typing test. The employment agency tested her at 50 words a minute. But Catherine knows that her keyboard skills are not that good.

Catherine has just entered the Ace Plumbing Supplies Company office. She is to be interviewed by Mr. Hervey, the owner.

Catherine and Mr. Hervey

Directions

- Use the photos to rate Catherine's grooming, clothing, posture, body control, and eye contact.
- As you read the interview, note Catherine's manners, language, personality, preparation, attitude, motivation, and qualifications. Also note the way she listens, the answers she gives, and the questions she asks.
- Underline any of Catherine's statements that may help her get the job. Circle any of Catherine's statements that may hurt her chances. Box any statements that may not be harmful but could be improved.

MR. HERVEY: Are you the girl from the Perfect Match Agency?

CATHERINE: Yes. I'm Catherine Morales. Are you Mr. Hervey?

MR. HERVEY: Yes. I was expecting you at 11:30. It's 12:15 now. I'm missing my lunch.

CATHERINE: Oh! I'm sorry. I didn't know it was so late. But I had to take two buses and I—

MR. HERVEY: Have a seat, Miss...

CATHERINE: Morales. Catherine Morales. How much time do people get for lunch here?

MR. HERVEY: They get an hour. But we can talk about that later. Did the agency tell you about the job?

CATHERINE: Not very much. Does it involve shorthand? I can't take shorthand.

MR. HERVEY: No. There is no shorthand. All we need is a general clerk—a clerk-typist. You can type, can't you? You should be able to type at least 50 words a minute.

CATHERINE: Uh...yes...I can type about 50 words a minute.

MR. HERVEY: We need someone to type out statements, letters, and things like that. Do some filing. Answer the telephone. Help me and the bookkeeper and the salesmen with whatever needs to be done.

CATHERINE: Who do you sell to?

MR. HERVEY: We sell mostly to construction companies and owners of buildings.

CATHERINE: That sounds interesting.

MR. HERVEY: Have you lived in River City very long?

CATHERINE: No. I just came here from Hillsdale. I'm living with two girl friends. They both got great jobs downtown with a bank. They are working in a really beautiful office.

MR. HERVEY: I suppose this place is not very exciting for a young girl to work in. You would probably be happier in an office downtown. A place with lots of other young people.

CATHERINE: Oh, I don't mind.

MR. HERVEY: The woman at the agency said that you didn't have any office experience. Do you think you could handle our files?

CATHERINE: I was wondering about the salary. The agency woman said it was only $180 a week. Do you give a raise after a while?

MR. HERVEY: That depends, Miss Morales. That depends.

CATHERINE: Some of the other places where I've been interviewed pay more.

MR. HERVEY: Well, that may be Miss Morales. Now if you have no more questions...

CATHERINE: I don't think so. Is there a ladies room here?

MR. HERVEY: Yes, there is. If you want to use it...

CATHERINE: No. I don't. Maybe I should just take a look at it though....No, that's all right.

MR. HERVEY: Thank you for coming in, Miss Morales.

CATHERINE: You're welcome. You know, this is not such a bad place after all. I think I would like to work here. But the salary is...Suppose I call you back in a few days to let you know how I feel about it?

MR. HERVEY: That won't be necessary. Just tell the woman at the Perfect Match Agency. Good-bye now.

CATHERINE: Yes, all right. Good-bye.

What Do You Think?

Rating the Applicant

A. Use the form below to show the kind of first impression Catherine made on you. See page 16 for directions.

```
┌─────────────────────────────────────────────┐
│             First Impressions                │
│                                               │
│ Scoring  Excellent......15  Fair........5     │
│          Good.........10   Poor........0      │
│                                               │
│  ┌──────────────────────┬──────────────┐     │
│  │        Item          │    Score     │     │
│  ├──────────────────────┼──────────────┤     │
│  │ Grooming             │              │     │
│  ├──────────────────────┼──────────────┤     │
│  │ Clothing             │              │     │
│  ├──────────────────────┼──────────────┤     │
│  │ Posture/Body Control │              │     │
│  ├──────────────────────┼──────────────┤     │
│  │ Eye Contact          │              │     │
│  ├──────────────────────┼──────────────┤     │
│  │ Manners              │              │     │
│  ├──────────────────────┼──────────────┤     │
│  │ Language             │              │     │
│  ├──────────────────────┼──────────────┤     │
│  │ Personality          │              │     │
│  ├──────────────────────┼──────────────┤     │
│  │               Total  │              │     │
│  └──────────────────────┴──────────────┘     │
│                                               │
│ Rating  ☐ Excellent 91–105  ☐ Fair ..31–65   │
│         ☐ Good ....66–90     ☐ Poor ..0–30    │
└─────────────────────────────────────────────┘
```

B. Rate Catherine on each item below. Be ready to explain your rating.
1. **Preparation** (Was Catherine well prepared for the interview?)
   ☐ Excellent   ☐ Fair
   ☐ Good   ☐ Poor
2. **Attitude** (Does Catherine seem mostly positive or negative about herself and the new job?)
   ☐ Excellent   ☐ Fair
   ☐ Good   ☐ Poor
3. **Motivation** (Does Catherine seem to really want the job?)
   ☐ Excellent   ☐ Fair
   ☐ Good   ☐ Poor
4. **Qualifications** (Does Catherine seem to have the abilities and experience to do well on the job?)
   ☐ Excellent   ☐ Fair
   ☐ Good   ☐ Poor

Rating, *Continued*

5. **Listening/Answering/Asking** (Does Catherine listen carefully, answer all questions fully, and ask important questions?)
   ☐ Excellent   ☐ Fair
   ☐ Good   ☐ Poor

Close-up on the Interview

A. Answer the questions below.
1. What should Catherine have done to make sure she could get to the interview on time?

   _____

   _____

   _____

2. What should she have done to be more certain of her keyboard skills?

   _____

   _____

   _____

3. Does Catherine seem to really want the job?
   ☐ Yes   ☐ No   Why or why not?

   _____

   _____

   _____

B. If you were Mr. Hervey, would you hire Catherine?
   ☐ Yes   ☐ No   Why or why not?

   _____

   _____

C. If you could talk to Catherine, what advice would you give her?

   _____

   _____

   _____

Bonus

Suppose an interviewer asked you to tell about the kind of work skills you have. What would you say?

Supermarket Clerk

The Job

A supermarket clerk may:
- mark prices of grocery items
- prepare, bag, weigh, and mark prices on fresh fruits and vegetables
- stock shelves
- bag groceries
- return shopping carts to cart stations
- keep floors clean
- take returned bottles to storeroom
- unload delivery trucks
- load customers' cars
- make home deliveries
- clean store after closing

Uniphoto

The Applicant

José Estevez is 20 years old. He is married and has a son nine months old. José has been out of school for two years. He has had two jobs during that time and has quit both. He is now looking for another job. One day he read this ad in the help-wanted section of the morning newspaper.

SUPERMARKET CLERKS

Clerks are now being hired
for our new store opening June 25
in the Oaktree Shopping Mall.

Must be over 18 and willing to
work nights and weekends.

Telephone 555-1900.

SUREWAY STORES, INC.

José called the number in the ad. He spoke with a man in the personnel department. The man took his name and address and sent José an application form.

José got the application form in the mail two days later. He completed it and sent it back that day. A week later, he got a call from Sureway Stores. The caller asked José to come in for an interview. He said to come to the Personnel Department, 811 Brannigan Street, at 2:00 p.m. on April 29th, to see Mrs. Higgins. José has just arrived.

José and Mrs. Higgins

Directions

- Use the photos to rate José's grooming, clothing, posture, body control and eye contact.
- As you read the interview, note José's manners, language, personality, preparation, attitude, motivation, and qualifications. Also note the way he listens, the answers he gives, and the questions he asks.
- <u>Underline</u> any of José's statements that may help him get the job. (Circle) any of José's statements that may hurt his chances. | Box | any statements that may not be harmful but could be improved.

MS. TAYLOR: Are you here to see Mrs. Higgins?

JOSÉ: Yes. I got a call telling me to come in for an interview at two.

MS. TAYLOR: Oh. You must be Mr. Estevez. But it's only one thirty.

JOSÉ: That's right. Am I too early? Should I come back later?

MS. TAYLOR: No. That's all right. Please take a seat over there with the others. I'll call you when Mrs. Higgins is ready to see you.

José sits with the others wating to see Mrs. Higgins. He chats with them. He finds they have better work experience that he does. They seem better qualified than him. By the time Mrs. Higgins is ready to see him, he is very nervous.

MS. TAYLOR: Mr. Estevez. You can go in now.

MRS. HIGGINS: How do you do, Mr. Estevez. I'm Martha Higgins. Please have a seat.

JOSÉ: Nice to meet you. Thank you. (He nervously puts out a hand for a handshake. Mrs. Higgins doesn't see it because she has started looking at José's application. He sits down.)

MRS. HIGGINS: I see that you graduated from East River City High School. How did you do there?

JOSÉ: Well, not too good. I wanted to drop out and go to work. But my mother wanted me to graduate. So I stayed on.

MRS. HIGGINS: I see. Then I don't suppose you plan to go back to school.

JOSÉ: Who, me? No. What good would that do me? I'm married and got a kid. I need a job. I need a job real bad, you see?

MRS. HIGGINS: Yes, I understand, Mr. Estevez. According to your job application form, you have had two jobs since you graduated from high school. Tell me about them.

JOSÉ: Well, they weren't too good. Not for me anyway. On the first one, I didn't get along too well with the boss. That was in the laundry. He was always complaining about me being late for work. But I couldn't help that. I had an old car. It kept breaking down. I had a long way to go.

MRS. HIGGINS: You were late a lot then?

JOSÉ: Yes, but it wasn't my fault.

MRS. HIGGINS: Were you fired for being late?

JOSÉ: Oh no! I quit that job. I wasn't making enough money. You can call them and see. Oh, no. They didn't fire me.

MRS. HIGGINS: How about the job with Aunt Polly's Jams and Jellies. You were there almost a year. What happened?

JOSÉ: Well…it was the people there, the old women. I didn't get along with them. They didn't like me. Always giving me a hard time, talking about me to the foreman…But the money wasn't bad, six fifty ($6.50) an hour. What are you paying here?

MRS. HIGGINS: The starting salary is six dollars ($6.00) an hour.

JOSÉ: I guess I could get by on that. You see, my wife works too. She's a waitress. Maybe she can get a job at Oaktree Mall. They must have some restaurants there. Then I could get a car and we could drive to work together.

MRS. HIGGINS: Don't you have a car now? The Oaktree Mall is in a new suburb, Woodmont. Public transportation is very poor. I don't think there is a night bus back to the city. And this is a night job we are talking about.

JOSÉ: Oh, don't worry. I'll find some way. Maybe I can meet someone who goes the same way. Later, I'll get a car. I really need this job bad, you know. I got a little kid, a boy. You want to see his picture?

What Do You Think? _____

Rating the Applicant

A. Use the form below to show the kind of first impression José made on you. See page 16 for directions.

First Impressions

Scoring Excellent 15   Fair 5
Good 10   Poor 0

Item	Score
Grooming	
Clothing	
Posture/Body Control	
Eye Contact	
Manners	
Language	
Personality	
Total	

Rating ☐ Excellent 91–105   ☐ Fair . . 31–65
☐ Good 66–90   ☐ Poor . . 0–30

B. Rate José on each item below. Be ready to explain your rating.

1. **Preparation** (Was José well prepared for the interview?)
   ☐ Excellent   ☐ Fair
   ☐ Good   ☐ Poor
2. **Attitude** (Does José seem mostly positive or negative about himself, his previous jobs, and the new job?)
   ☐ Excellent   ☐ Fair
   ☐ Good   ☐ Poor
3. **Motivation** (Does José seem to really want the job?)
   ☐ Excellent   ☐ Fair
   ☐ Good   ☐ Poor
4. **Qualifications** (Does José seem to have the abilities and experience to do well on the job?)
   ☐ Excellent   ☐ Fair
   ☐ Good   ☐ Poor

Rating, *Continued*

5. **Listening/Answering/Asking** (Does José listen carefully, answer all questions fully, and ask important questions?)
   ☐ Excellent   ☐ Fair
   ☐ Good   ☐ Poor

Close-up on the Interview

A. Fill in the word that best completes each sentence.

along   before   nervous   skills

1. Getting to the interview too early and talking to the other applicants made José more _____.
2. José's problems with his previous boss and co-workers makes it seem as though he can't get _____ with people at work.
3. José should have talked more about the _____ he learned on his previous jobs.
4. José should have figured out exactly how he would get to the new job _____ he went for the interview.

B. If you were Mrs. Higgins, would you hire José?
   ☐ Yes   ☐ No   Why or why not?

_____
_____
_____
_____

C. If you could talk to José, what advice would you give him?

_____
_____
_____

Bonus

Suppose an interviewer asked you the questions below. What would you say?
1. How did you do in school?
2. How did you do on your last job?

Dining Room Attendant

The Job

A dining room attendant may:
- carry dirty dishes, silverware, and glasses from dining room to kitchen
- replace dirty table linens and set tables
- serve water, bread, and butter to customers
- keep a supply of linens, dishes, silverware, and glasses in dining room
- supply service areas with food
- keep service areas and equipment clean
- run errands and deliver food orders

The Applicant

Alan "Chip" Roberts graduated from high school a month ago. He has been answering ads in the newspaper. So far he has not found a job.

One day, Chip's neighbor told him he should try the State Employment Office. A counselor there told him that all the jobs they had could be found listed on the bulletin board. She told him to tell her if he saw anything he wanted.

Chip read all the job notices. He decided to try for this job:

Dining Room Attendant

Clean off tables in restaurant. Over 18, good health, clean-cut appearance. 40-hour week. $4.00 an hour plus tips. No experience necessary.

The counselor called the employer. She told him about Chip. The employer said he was interested in meeting Chip. So, an interview was scheduled.

The counselor gave Chip a piece of paper. On the paper was written the time, 3:30 p.m., that Chip was to see Mr. Griffin, the owner of the Hickory Shack Restaurant. The paper also gave the address of the restaurant, the name of the job, the hours, and the salary. Chip is being interviewed now.

Chip and Mr. Griffin

Directions

- Use the photos to rate Chip's grooming, clothing, posture, body control, and eye contact.
- As you read the interview, note Chip's manners, language, personality, preparation, attitude, motivation, and qualifications. Also note the way he listens, the answers he gives, and the questions he asks.
- Underline any of Chip's statements that may help him get the job. Circle any of Chip's statements that may hurt his chances. Box any statements that may not be harmful but could be improved.

MR. GRIFFIN: So you have never worked in a restaurant before?

CHIP: No.

MR. GRIFFIN: Have you ever had any kind of a job?

CHIP: Oh, sure. I've had some part-time and summer jobs.

MR. GRIFFIN: Tell me about them. What did you do?

CHIP: Well, my last job was with Stanton's Department Store. I liked it at first. But then the manager started picking on me all the time. He used to work my tail off. Always watching me. Didn't want me talking or anything. So I quit.

MR. GRIFFIN: How long did you work at Stanton's?

CHIP: A few days? Last summer I had a job in Lakeview Park. That was a great job. No one bothering me all the time. A lot of the guys from school worked there. We had a ball!

MR. GRIFFIN: What were you doing?

CHIP: We had this—oh, you mean on the job? Well, we were supposed to keep the camping areas clean. You know, pick up papers and bottles. Things like that.

MR. GRIFFIN: Were you there all summer?

CHIP: No, not all summer. They found out they had hired too many of us. They had to let me and some of the other guys go.

MR. GRIFFIN: What was the longest time you ever held a job?

CHIP: Let me see. It must have been my newspaper route. Yeah, the paper route. I did that for a year or so. In the mornings. I would have kept it too. But Dad didn't like it. (He laughs.) He used to say that he ended up delivering papers more often than I did.

MR. GRIFFIN: How is your health?

CHIP: Good, I guess. No problems. (He laughs.)

MR. GRIFFIN: I mean, is there any reason you can't do this kind of work? Standing for hours, and lifting things?

CHIP: No. Not me. Say, you have any rules about eating things here?

MR. GRIFFIN: You get lunch and dinner here, if that's what you mean. That's like part of the salary.

CHIP: Yeah. And how about the tips? How does that work?

MR. GRIFFIN: The tips are collected for all the waitresses and attendants. They are divided later.

CHIP: Evenly?

MR. GRIFFIN: No. The attendants get 20%. Now let's get back to you. What makes you think you would like to work here?

CHIP: Well, Mr. Griffin, it's this way. I want a job. And I think I could do OK at the Hickory Shack.

MR. GRIFFIN: All right, Chip. If you have no more questions about the job…

CHIP: No. It seems pretty simple to me. Oh yeah, one thing. Would it be all right if I took a week off in August? I mean, if I get the job. You see, my aunt and uncle always let me stay with them for a week at their house on the lake. I would hate to miss it.

MR. GRIFFIN: Well, I'll see, Chip. I'll see.

CHIP: When will you let me know about the job? You want me to call you?

MR. GRIFFIN: No. I'll be in touch with you by the end of the week. Good-bye, Chip.

CHIP: All right. So long, Mr. Griffin.

What Do You Think?

Rating the Applicant

A. Use the form below to show the kind of first impression Chip made on you. See page 16 for directions.

```
┌─────────────────────────────────────────────┐
│              First Impressions                │
│                                               │
│  Scoring  Excellent.......15   Fair........5  │
│           Good .........10   Poor........0    │
├────────────────────────┬──────────────────────┤
│         Item           │        Score          │
├────────────────────────┼──────────────────────┤
│  Grooming              │                       │
├────────────────────────┼──────────────────────┤
│  Clothing              │                       │
├────────────────────────┼──────────────────────┤
│  Posture/Body Control  │                       │
├────────────────────────┼──────────────────────┤
│  Eye Contact           │                       │
├────────────────────────┼──────────────────────┤
│  Manners               │                       │
├────────────────────────┼──────────────────────┤
│  Language              │                       │
├────────────────────────┼──────────────────────┤
│  Personality           │                       │
├────────────────────────┼──────────────────────┤
│              Total     │                       │
└────────────────────────┴──────────────────────┘
  Rating  ☐ Excellent 91–105   ☐ Fair . .31–65
          ☐ Good ....66–90     ☐ Poor . .0–30
```

B. Rate Chip on each item below. Be ready to explain your rating.

1. **Preparation** (Was Chip well prepared for the interview?)
   ☐ Excellent   ☐ Fair
   ☐ Good   ☐ Poor

2. **Attitude** (Does Chip seem mostly positive or negative about himself, his previous jobs, and the new job?)
   ☐ Excellent   ☐ Fair
   ☐ Good   ☐ Poor

3. **Motivation** (Does Chip seem to really want the job?)
   ☐ Excellent   ☐ Fair
   ☐ Good   ☐ Poor

4. **Qualifications** (Does Chip seem to have the abilities and experience to do well on the job?)
   ☐ Excellent   ☐ Fair
   ☐ Good   ☐ Poor

Rating, *Continued*

5. **Listening/Answering/Asking** (Does Chip listen carefully, answer all questions fully, and ask important questions?)
   ☐ Excellent   ☐ Fair
   ☐ Good   ☐ Poor

Close-up on the Interview

A. Write **T** if the statement is true. Write **F** if it is false. Be ready to explain your answer.

___ 1. Chip's appearance, manners, and posture are all suitable for a job as a dining room attendant.

___ 2. The things Chip tells about his work history make it seem as though he would be a good worker.

___ 3. Chip asks some good questions but at the wrong time.

___ 4. Chip gives a poor reason for wanting to work at the Hickory Shack.

B. If you were Mr. Griffin, would you hire Chip?
☐ Yes   ☐ No   Why or why not?

_____

_____

_____

_____

_____

C. If you could talk to Chip, what advice would you give him?

_____

_____

_____

_____

_____

Bonus

Imagine you are applying for a job at the Hickory Shack. Mr. Griffin asks you why you would like to work there. What are some reasons you might give?

Electronics Assembler

The Job

An electronics assembler may:
- assemble electronic equipment, such as computers and tape recorders
- use electronic test equipment and hand and power tools
- follow blueprints, wiring diagrams, and the like
- test complete assembly and make necessary repairs

Photo courtesy of Hewlett-Packard Company

The Applicant

Evelyn Petersen never made plans about working when she was in school. "I'll just take any job," she thought, "until I meet some great guy and get married. Then I'll have a family and won't have to worry about a job."

Evelyn got a job as soon as she graduated. She sorted and boxed clothes in a warehouse. She did meet a guy and she did get married. She quit her job and had a baby girl.

Everything was fine for about a year. But then Evelyn's husband left her. He just disappeared.

Evelyn went on welfare and got a divorce. She tried to find a job through the State Employment Office and private agencies. But they all said she had no "marketable skills."

The jobs Evelyn could get, after deductions and baby-sitting fees, paid less than welfare. But one Sunday, Evelyn saw this ad in the newspaper and got very excited.

Electronics assembler   No exp. nec. Must be good at detail work. Company ben. incl. child care. $4.90 hr. Apply Pers. Dept., Tecudex Industries, 27977 Industrial Way, River City

Evelyn has just arrived at Tecudex.

Evelyn, Ms. Sharp, and Mr. Warner _____

Directions

- Use the photos to rate Evelyn's grooming, clothing, posture, body control, and eye contact.
- As you read the interview, note Evelyn's manners, language, personality, preparation, attitude, motivation, and qualifications. Also note the way she listens, the answers she gives, and the questions she asks.
- <u>Underline</u> any of Evelyn's statements that may help her get the job. (Circle) any of Evelyn's statements that may hurt her chances. [Box] any statements that may not be harmful but could be improved.

EVELYN: Hello. I'm here to see about the job that was in Sunday's paper.

MS. SHARP: Which position was that? We had several ads.

Evelyn's baby, Lisa, pulls on her mother's arm.

EVELYN: Stop that Lisa! Be still while Mommy talks to the lady....It was for assemblers, electronic assemblers. I'd like to put my name in.

MS. SHARP: Certainly. Just take a seat over there with the others and fill out this application.

EVELYN: Can't I just take it with me and mail it back? I just thought I could drop in and find out about the job.

MS. SHARP: I'm sorry. But Mr. Warner wants all of the applicants to complete the forms today.

EVELYN: Oh, all right. Now Lisa, be a good girl for Mommy.

Evelyn sits at a table and fills out the form. Lisa pesters her and she has to scold the child. Finally she finishes the form and returns it to Ms. Sharp.

EVELYN: Miss, here is my application. I couldn't fill it all out. I don't have some of the addresses with me. Is that all right?

MS. SHARP: Don't worry about it, Mrs. Petersen. Please take a seat with the others. Mr. Warner will be giving the aptitude test in about half an hour.

EVELYN: Test? I can't. I mean—you didn't say anything about testing in your newspaper ad.

MS. SHARP: Well, you must understand, Mrs. Petersen. We can't say everything in one small ad. If you can't take the test this morning, you can come back this afternoon. The second testing will be at 4:00 p.m.

EVELYN: Oh boy…I borrowed a neighbor's car to get down here. I don't have a car. I won't be able to come back this afternoon.

MS. SHARP: I'll tell you what, Mrs. Petersen. Why don't you take your little girl to our Child Care Center? Then you can be free to take the test.

EVELYN: Oh, that's great! Tell me how to find it. Oh, and where is the ladies room?

Ms. Sharp tells Evelyn how to find the Child Care Center. Evelyn takes Lisa there. Then she goes to the ladies room and fixes her hair. Next she takes the test. Soon she is called to see Mr. Warner. She starts talking before he says anything.

EVELYN: I know I didn't do well. I hope you will understand. I didn't come prepared for testing this morning. I had to bring my little girl and…

MR. WARNER: Relax, Mrs. Petersen. You did OK on the test. Otherwise I wouldn't have called you in.

EVELYN: Really?

MR. WARNER: Really. So please sit down and tell me why you want this job.

EVELYN: (sitting down) Well…I…it's like a dream. The pay is very good. You don't need experience. There's child care—

MR. WARNER: What about the work itself? Do you think you would like to be an electronic assembler?

EVELYN: Well, I don't know exactly what an electronic assembler does. But your ad said something about detail work. My friends tell me I'm good with details.

MR. WARNER: Yes, your test shows you have an aptitude in that area. Tell me about the job you had before you got married. What kind of worker would you say you were?

EVELYN: Well, I think I was a good worker. I mean, I always finished my work on time. I was never late for work. My boss said he was sorry to see me go.

MR. WARNER: And why did you leave?

EVELYN: To get married and have a baby.

MR. WARNER: I see. And how long do you think you might keep this job if you are hired?

EVELYN: Oh, for a long time. You see, I'm divorced and need to support myself and my child.

What Do You Think?

Rating the Applicant

A. Use the form below to show the kind of first impression Evelyn made on you. See page 16 for directions.

First Impressions

Scoring Excellent.......15   Fair.......5
Good........10   Poor.......0

Item	Score
Grooming	
Clothing	
Posture/Body Control	
Eye Contact	
Manners	
Language	
Personality	
Total	

Rating ☐ Excellent 91–105   ☐ Fair . . 31–65
☐ Good 66–90   ☐ Poor . . 0–30

B. Rate Evelyn on each item below. Be ready to explain your rating.

1. **Preparation** (Was Evelyn well prepared for the interview?)
   ☐ Excellent   ☐ Fair
   ☐ Good   ☐ Poor
2. **Attitude** (Does Evelyn seem mostly positive or negative about herself, her previous job, and the new job?)
   ☐ Excellent   ☐ Fair
   ☐ Good   ☐ Poor
3. **Motivation** (Does Evelyn seem to really want the job?)
   ☐ Excellent   ☐ Fair
   ☐ Good   ☐ Poor
4. **Qualifications** (Does Evelyn seem to have the abilities and experience to do well on the job?)
   ☐ Excellent   ☐ Fair
   ☐ Good   ☐ Poor

Rating, *Continued*

5. **Listening/Answering/Asking** (Does Evelyn listen carefully, answer all questions fully, and ask important questions?)
   ☐ Excellent   ☐ Fair
   ☐ Good   ☐ Poor

Close-up on the Interview

A. Fill in the word that best completes each sentence.

aptitude	dressed
child	interview

1. Evelyn should have been prepared to fill out a job application, take a test, and have an _____.
2. She should have _____ in a suitable manner.
3. Evelyn should not have brought her _____ along.
4. The only reason Evelyn was called in for an interview was that she did OK on the _____ test.

B. If you were Mr. Warner, would you hire Evelyn? ☐ Yes   ☐ No   Why or why not?

_____

_____

_____

_____

C. If you could talk to Evelyn, what advice would you give her?

_____

_____

_____

_____

Bonus

Suppose an interviewer asked you to tell why you left your last job and any other jobs you have had. What would you say?

Fish Wholesaler's Assistant

The Job

A fish wholesaler's assistant may:

- receive and inspect deliveries of fish
- read customers' orders for number, size, and kind of fish
- pick out fish, weigh them, and record their weight
- clean and fillet fish
- assemble boxes
- pack fish in boxes with ice
- label boxes with names and addresses of customers
- drive a forklift
- load boxes on truck
- deliver boxes to stores, restaurants, hospitals, airports, and other places
- get customers to sign for deliveries

The Applicant

Ted Johnson lives in Seaside, a summer resort and fishing center not far from River City. He has worked every summer since he was 14. And he has had several different part-time jobs after school and on weekends.

Now that Ted has graduated from high school he wants a full time job. He has a license to drive a small truck. He thinks he might get a job as a driver.

Ted tells everyone he knows that he is looking for a job. But he keeps looking, too. Every day he goes to different places of business. Ted spends most of his time down at the docks.

The Seaside docks are where the fishing boats tie up. The catch is sold there, mostly to the canneries and

frozen food processors. Most businesses connected with the fishing industry are to be found in the docks area.

Morning is busy at the Seaside docks. Ted makes it a point to be there early. He is now outside the Tambellini Brothers warehouse. He is talking to Dominic Tambellini about getting a job.

Ted and the Tambellini Brothers

Directions

- Use the photos to rate Ted's grooming, clothing, posture, body control, and eye contact.
- As you read the interview, note Ted's manners, language, personality, preparation, attitude, motivation, and qualifications. Also note the way he listens, the answers he gives, and the questions he asks.
- Underline any of Ted's statements that may help him get the job. Circle any of Ted's statements that may hurt his chances. Box any statements that may not be harmful but could be improved.

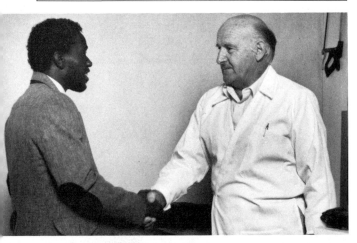

D. TAMBELLINI: Weren't you in here before?

TED: Yes, Mr. Tambellini. I was in here about two weeks ago. I'm still looking for work.

D. TAMBELLINI: I would think that a strong young man like you would be able to find a job.

TED: It's not easy, Mr. Tambellini. I guess things are pretty tight here in Seaside these days.

D. TAMBELLINI: Jobs are always tight here. Just ask my brother Angelo and me. We've always had to do everything ourselves to make a dollar here.

TED: Didn't your sons work for you before they moved to River City? You must need a helper. Why don't you give me a job? You and your brother are not getting any younger. How about it?

D. TAMBELLINI: Give, give, give. That's all I hear these days from young people. All you want is give. Angelo, you have to hear this one. This kid thinks we're ready to retire.

A. TAMBELLINI: What is this about retiring? You want me to go buy some golf clubs and fishing poles, Dominic?

D. TAMBELLINI: He does, not me. He thinks we should give him a job. What do you say, Angelo?

A. TAMBELLINI: I'm not so sure. What did we say last time, Mr....?

TED: Ted Johnson. Last time I was in here you said you would think about taking me on as a helper, remember?

D. TAMBELLINI: Yes, I guess we did say that, didn't we?

A. TAMBELLINI: I think he looks too businesslike for this job. He won't be able to wear his good clothes here. What do you think, Dominic?

D. TAMBELLINI: If we get a helper, one of us won't have to drive the truck to River City. He can do all the fish packing, too. He could do a lot of things around here.

TED: I have a license to drive a truck, Mr. Tambellini. And I can pack fish with the best of them!

D. TAMBELLINI: If you pack for us, you would be packing with the best.

A. TAMBELLINI: What kind of work have you done before?

TED: I've done just about everything you can do in Seaside for part-time and summer work. For the past two summers, I worked in the kitchen of the Seaside Lodge. Before that, I worked summers at Harley's Restaurant as a dining room attendant. And I've had part-time jobs in gas stations, stores, delivering newspapers—you name it.

D. TAMBELLINI: Suppose we tried you out. You know, working here packing fish, making deliveries in River City. What rate of pay would you need?

TED: Well, Mr. Tambellini, that's up to you. I was making about $180 a week at the Lodge.

D. TAMBELLINI: Oh, you worked for Lipski at the Lodge? Would he give you a good reference if we call him?

TED: Yes, I'm sure he would.

D. TAMBELLINI: Well, we'll think about it, Ted. We'll talk together later and then we'll call you. Write your phone number here.

TED: Thank you, Mr. Tambellini. I really appreciate it. Do you mind if I call you tomorrow, instead? You see, I'm usually out most of the time looking for work.

D. TAMBELLINI: Sure. You give us a call tomorrow. We'll talk to you then.

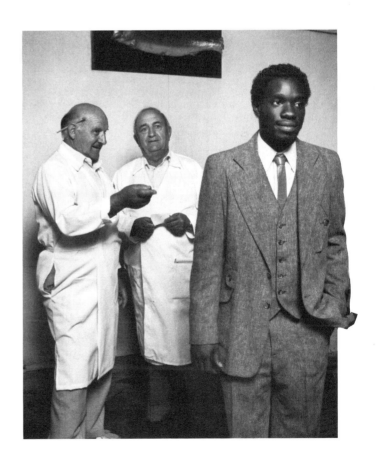

What Do You Think?

Rating the Applicant

A. Use the form below to show the kind of first impression Ted made on you. See page 16 for directions.

First Impressions

Scoring Excellent......15 Fair.......5
Good ....10 Poor........0

Item	Score
Grooming	
Clothing	
Posture/Body Control	
Eye Contact	
Manners	
Language	
Personality	
Total	

Rating ☐ Excellent 91–105 ☐ Fair . . 31–65
☐ Good . . . . 66–90 ☐ Poor . . 0–30

B. Rate Ted on each item below. Be ready to explain your rating.
1. **Preparation** (Was Ted well prepared for the interview?)
   ☐ Excellent ☐ Fair
   ☐ Good ☐ Poor
2. **Attitude** (Does Ted seem mostly positive or negative about himself, his previous jobs, and the new job?)
   ☐ Excellent ☐ Fair
   ☐ Good ☐ Poor
3. **Motivation** (Does Ted seem to really want the job?)
   ☐ Excellent ☐ Fair
   ☐ Good ☐ Poor
4. **Qualifications** (Does Ted seem to have the abilities and experience to do well on the job?)
   ☐ Excellent ☐ Fair
   ☐ Good ☐ Poor

Rating, *Continued*

5. **Listening/Answering/Asking** (Does Ted listen carefully, answer all questions fully, and ask important questions?)
   ☐ Excellent ☐ Fair
   ☐ Good ☐ Poor

Close-up on the Interview

A. Underline three things below that could be helpful for Ted to do.
  a. He should be more polite.
  b. He should get letters of recommendation from people he has worked for.
  c. He should dress to suit the place where the interview is to take place.
  d. He should be more sure of himself.
  e. He should decide how much he wants to get paid.

B. If you were one of the Tambellini brothers, would you hire Ted? ☐ Yes ☐ No
Why or why not?

_____

_____

_____

_____

_____

C. If you could talk to Ted, what advice would you give him?

_____

_____

_____

_____

Bonus

Suppose an interviewer asked you to answer the questions below. What would you say?
1. How much do you need to get paid per week after deductions?
2. Would you accept part-time or temporary work?

Hospital Attendant

The Job

A hospital attendant may:
• carry food and drink to patients
• feed, wash, and dress patients
• make beds and replace room supplies
• deliver and set up equipment
• clean rooms

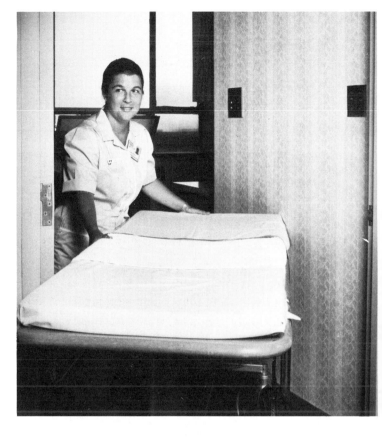

The Applicant

Pete Sandoval is finishing a four-month course for hospital attendants given at Jefferson Community College. He is ready now to look for a job.

Pete has filled out job applications at local hospitals and nursing homes. He has listed his name with several agencies that attended the Job Fair at his community college. And he has answered two ads that appeared in the newspaper.

Pete has already had a few job interviews at hospitals and rest homes. Since most of the places have the same union for attendants—the salaries, hours, and benefits are the same. The working

conditions, though, can be quite different from place to place.

Pete has been called in for an interview at Mercy General Hospital. The personnel department has sent him to see the head nurse, Mrs. Ethel Burnett.

Pete and Mrs. Burnett

Directions

- Use the photos to rate Pete's grooming, clothing, posture, body control, and eye contact.
- As you read the interview, note Pete's manners, language, personality, preparation, attitude, motivation, and qualifications. Also note the way he listens, the answers he gives, and the questions he asks.
- Underline any of Pete's statements that may help him get the job. Circle any of Pete's statements that may hurt his chances. Box any statements that may not be harmful but could be improved.

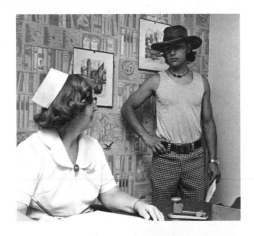

PETE: Hello. Are you the head nurse? I'm Pete Sandoval. You know, the personnel lady told me to come see you.

MRS. BURNETT: Yes, Mr. Sandoval. Mrs. Washington told me she was sending you down. Please take a seat. (She waits for Pete to sit down.) Mrs. Washington tells me that you are finishing a course for attendants at Jefferson Community College.

PETE: Yeah, that's right. You know, I thought it was going to be a hard course. But it was real easy for me. This Internal Medicine Department—do you run the whole thing?

MRS. BURNETT: I'm the head nurse. The nursing staff and attendants are under me.

PETE: That's really something, you know. Well, Mrs. Washington said this was the department that needed a new attendant the most. How come? No one like to work here?

MRS. BURNETT: We are very busy in this department, Mr. Sandoval. Our patients need more care and attention than on some of the other floors. And we need more help at night.

PETE: Yeah! She told me that. I told her I didn't think I would go for night work, you know. I've been to other hospitals, you know. They've been talking to me about jobs too.

MRS. BURNETT: Yes, I'm sure, Mr. Sandoval. Now suppose you tell me why you are interested in being an attendant at Mercy Hospital.

PETE: I've been to five hospitals already. I think I'll get a job easy. But I got to find the best place for me, you know?

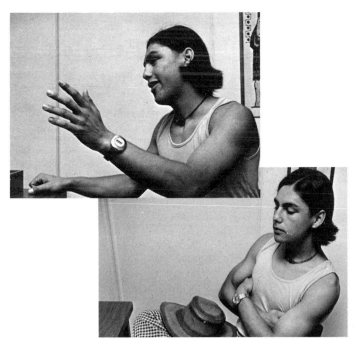

MRS. BURNETT: Yes. Well, I know the Jefferson course is a good one. But we do have other staff members to think about. New attendants are always put on the night shift.

PETE: What are the hours here for the night shift?

MRS. BURNETT: Twelve to eight in the morning.

PETE: Say, I don't know if I could take that, you know. I have to have a little social life, you know.

MRS. BURNETT: (Getting upset.) Mr. Sandoval, I don't think you quite understand the situation. If you are a good worker, we would like to have you here. But new attendants start out on the night shift. And that's it. Now if you don't want to do that then we have nothing more to discuss.

PETE: Oh, well, no harm trying, you know. I guess I could get used to it. Maybe go to the beach in the daytime. But let's get to the thing about the cleaning. That personnel woman said I would have to do cleaning up. I mean, you know, I didn't go to school for that.

MRS. BURNETT: Mr. Sandoval, I don't think you understood Mrs. Washington. Attendants may be called on to clean patients' rooms. It does not happen very often. But if we are short-handed, attendants have to help. Now perhaps you can tell me why you want to work in a hospital.

PETE: Oh sure. Well, it's good money, you know. I mean, it pays better than other jobs I thought about.

MRS. BURNETT: I see. And how do you feel about working with sick people?

PETE: That don't bother me. My grandfather used to live with us. He was always sick, you know. I had to help clean him up, get him dressed, stuff like that. Say, I have to buy my own uniforms, huh?

MRS. BURNETT: That's right, Mr. Sandoval. That's the same in all hospitals. Now what other kinds of work—

PETE: Can I get them cleaned here in the hospital? I mean free? I have to think of these things, you know?

What Do You Think?

Rating the Applicant

A. Use the form below to show the kind of first impression Pete made on you. See page 16 for directions.

See page 16 for directions.

First Impressions

Scoring Excellent 15   Fair 5
Good 10   Poor 0

Item	Score
Grooming	
Clothing	
Posture/Body Control	
Eye Contact	
Manners	
Language	
Personality	
Total	

Rating ☐ Excellent 91–105   ☐ Fair . . 31–65
☐ Good 66–90   ☐ Poor . . 0–30

B. Rate Pete on each item below. Be ready to explain your rating.

1. **Preparation** (Was Pete well prepared for the interview?)
   ☐ Excellent   ☐ Fair
   ☐ Good   ☐ Poor

2. **Attitude** (Does Pete seem mostly positive or negative about himself and the new job?)
   ☐ Excellent   ☐ Fair
   ☐ Good   ☐ Poor

3. **Motivation** (Does Pete seem to really want the job?)
   ☐ Excellent   ☐ Fair
   ☐ Good   ☐ Poor

4. **Qualifications** (Does Pete seem to have the abilities and experience to do well on the job?)
   ☐ Excellent   ☐ Fair
   ☐ Good   ☐ Poor

Rating, *Continued*

5. **Listening/Answering/Asking** (Does Pete listen carefully, answer all questions fully, and ask important questions?)
   ☐ Excellent   ☐ Fair
   ☐ Good   ☐ Poor

Close-up on the Interview

A. Write **T** if the statement is true. Write **F** if it is false. Be ready to explain your answer.
   ___ 1. Pete's training and his experience with his grandfather could help him get a job as a hospital attendant.
   ___ 2. Pete's appearance and manners are also helpful.
   ___ 3. Pete is being very unreasonable about working night shifts.
   ___ 4. Pete's questions show that he thinks about the needs of others.

B. If you were Mrs. Burnett, would you hire Pete?
   ☐ Yes   ☐ No   Why or Why not?

   _____

   _____

   _____

   _____

   _____

C. If you could talk to Pete, what advice would you give him?

   _____

   _____

   _____

   _____

Bonus

Suppose an interviewer asked you how you feel about working at night and on weekends. What would you say?

Fast Food Worker

The Job

A fast food worker may:

- Take and fill orders for food
- Take payment and make change
- Use a point-of-sales computer terminal to register sales
- Prepare and cook food according to exact company directions
- Bring food orders to customers
- Set up and service salad bars
- Clear and clean tables

The Applicant

Betty Duval is looking for her first job. She is having trouble finding a job because she believes she has no skills or work experience. She is also a little shy. She feels nervous when she has to meet people for the first time.

Betty has been doing most of her job hunting through the newspaper help-wanted ads. But the few answers she received said that she didn't have the right qualifications.

One day, while she was out shopping, Betty saw a sign in the window of her favorite fast food restaurant. It said:

Hiring now!
Inquire within.

Betty walked around the block three times getting up the courage to go in.

Finally, before she could change her mind, she walked right up to the counter and asked if she could see the person who was doing the hiring.

She was introduced to Mr. Kendall Chou, the daytime manager. He asked her to fill out an application and let him know when she was done. She is now being interviewed by Mr. Chou.

Betty and Mr. Chou

Directions

- Use the photos to rate Betty's grooming, clothing, posture, body control, and eye contact.
- As you read the interview, note Betty's manners, language, personality, preparation, attitude, motivation, and qualifications. Also note the way she listens, the answers she gives, and the questions she asks.
- <u>Underline</u> any of Betty's statements that may help her get the job. (Circle) any of Betty's statements that may hurt her chances. | Box | any statements that may not be harmful but could be improved.

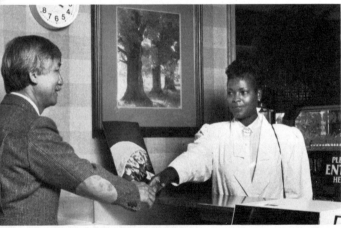

MR. CHOU: I see you left the work experience section of your application blank. Have you never had a job before?

BETTY: No. Well...not a paying job anyway.

MR. CHOU: Have you done some volunteer work?

BETTY: Yes.

MR. CHOU: Why don't you tell me about that?

BETTY: Well, I sold stuff at the church fair for the last couple of years. Sometimes I took care of the game booths. Sometimes I sold hot dogs. You know, stuff like that.

MR. CHOU: So you have handled money.

BETTY: Yes.

MR. CHOU: And did you do OK? I mean any trouble making change?

BETTY: No.

MR. CHOU: Wouldn't matter with our computer registers anyway. They tell you how much change to give....How did you feel about dealing with people?

BETTY: OK, I guess. I mean, I knew a lot of them from church.

MR. CHOU: Have you ever done any cooking?

BETTY: Oh sure. My mother works. So I've been getting supper ready for years. I also help prepare church suppers.

MR. CHOU: Well, Betty, it looks like you have some experience after all...Tell me, why would you like to work for Sandy's?

BETTY: Well, I need a job. I like working with food. So this seems like a good place to start. Could I be a cook here?

MR. CHOU: Yes, if we hired you, you would do some cooking. But we like people to be able to work the counter also. That way they can work wherever they are needed most. How would you feel about working the counter?

BETTY: Well…uh…I guess I could get used to it. Is the pay the same for both jobs?

MR. CHOU: Yes. Starting pay is four dollars and twenty-five cents ($4.25) an hour.

BETTY: (Disappointed) Oh…Does it go up?

MR CHOU: Top pay now is six fifty ($6.50) an hour. To get that you need to be able to do whatever needs to be done around here with no one telling you how to do it.

BETTY: How long does it take to earn that much money?

MR. CHOU: Well, we have one fellow who did it in about a year and a half.

BETTY: Do you get any benefits on this job?

MR. CHOU: Yes. After six months you get health and dental benefits…So, what do you think? Would you like to work for Sandy's?

BETTY: Yes, Mr. Chou, I would.

MR. CHOU: Well fine. We'll have to check out your references. You'll hear from us in a few days. If you don't, drop by or give me a call.

BETTY: OK. Thank you, Mr. Chou. I'm really glad I came in here.

MR. CHOU: You're welcome.

What Do You Think?

Rating the Applicant

A. Use the form below to show the kind of first impression Betty made on you. See page 16 for directions.

First Impressions

Scoring Excellent.......15 Fair 5
Good ....10 Poor 0

Item	Score
Grooming	
Clothing	
Posture/Body Control	
Eye Contact	
Manners	
Language	
Personality	
Total	

Rating ☐ Excellent 91–105 ☐ Fair ..31–65
☐ Good ....66–90 ☐ Poor ..0–30

B. Rate Betty on each item below. Be ready to explain your rating.
1. **Preparation** (Was Betty well prepared for the interview?)
   ☐ Excellent ☐ Fair
   ☐ Good ☐ Poor
2. **Attitude** (Does Betty seem mostly positive or negative about herself, her experience, and the new job?)
   ☐ Excellent ☐ Fair
   ☐ Good ☐ Poor
3. **Motivation** (Does Betty seem to really want the job?)
   ☐ Excellent ☐ Fair
   ☐ Good ☐ Poor
4. **Qualifications** (Does Betty seem to have the abilities and experience to do well on the job?)
   ☐ Excellent ☐ Fair
   ☐ Good ☐ Poor

Rating, *Continued*

5. **Listening/Answering/Asking** (Does Betty listen carefully, answer all questions fully, and ask important questions?)
   ☐ Excellent ☐ Fair
   ☐ Good ☐ Poor

Close-up on the Interview

A. Fill in the word that best completes each sentence.
   reasonable money home unpaid
   1. Betty's _____ work experience made a good impression on Mr. Chou.
   2. Mr. Chou was impressed with Betty's experience as a cook at _____ and in her church.
   3. Her experience selling things at church fairs shows she has experience handling
      _____.
   4. Betty is willing to work the counter even though she would rather be a cook. This shows she is a _____ person.

B. If you were Mr. Chou, would you hire Betty?
   ☐ Yes ☐ No Why or why not?

   _____

   _____

   _____

C. If you could talk to Betty, what advice would you give her?

   _____

   _____

   _____

Bonus

Suppose an interviewer asked you the questions below. What would you say?
1. What kind of unpaid work experience do you have?
2. How do you feel about handling money?
3. How good are you at dealing with people?

Paving Construction Worker

The Job

A paving construction worker may:
- sweep dirt away before asphalt is poured
- direct dump trucks to unloading point and let out asphalt
- scrape off asphalt that sticks to truck
- signal driver to move on
- spread asphalt evenly
- press asphalt flat in places road roller can't reach
- put up and take down road blocks

The Applicant

Last year Patrick Sweeney was arrested and convicted for selling drugs. He was selling to support his own habit. The judge offered Pat probation instead of prison, if he would take part in a drug treatment program.

Pat agreed to the program. He kicked the habit, and has been clean ever since. But he's having a hard time finding a job. He's been able to pick up temporary jobs here and there. But any time there is a job application with questions about convictions, he misses out. Interviewers see that he was convicted for selling drugs and never even call him in for an interview.

Pat told his probation officer, Mr. Ambrose, about the trouble he was

having. Mr. Ambrose gave Pat an idea about how to get around the problem.

Now Pat has gotten his first interview. He's applying for a job he heard about from a friend. It is with the National Paving Company. His interviewer is the company's manager, Mr. Smathers.

Pat and Mr. Smathers

MR. SMATHERS: Sweeney, you have had a lot of different jobs. But you never stay long at any of them. How come?

PAT: They were temporary jobs, Mr. Smathers. All except the one for Fox Protective Service. I was a guard. They let me go because I couldn't get a bond.

MR. SMATHERS: Couldn't get bonded?

PAT: No sir, and I'd like to explain that if I may. It's connected with what I wrote in the convictions box on the application form.

MR. SMATHERS: You wrote "to be explained in the interview."

PAT: Right. You see, I thought it would be better if I could meet you man to man and explain what happened to me.

MR. SMATHERS: OK, Sweeney. Start explaining.

PAT: Well, I used to be pretty heavy into drugs. And I was selling to support my habit. I got caught and was given a choice of prison or a treatment program. I took the treatment program. But the conviction stays on my record.

MR. SMATHERS: And the bonding company found out about the conviction?

PAT: That's right. They wouldn't bond me, so I lost the job.

MR. SMATHERS: When did you finish the treatment program?

PAT: About six months ago. I lived in a half-way house for awhile. But now I'm back with my family.

MR. SMATHERS: And you never...I mean you no longer feel the need to...?

PAT: To take drugs? I'm not going to lie to you, Mr. Smathers. Sure I sometimes feel the need. But I have control of that need now. I have a support group to turn to for help when I feel that need.

MR. SMATHERS: You know, Sweeney, you don't have much going for you. Why should we hire you? There are lots of people looking for jobs like this. Why should we take a chance on you?

PAT: Sir, all I can say is that I'll try harder. Harder than anyone else you could hire. I understand now what I was doing to myself, and I don't want to go back to my old ways.

MR. SMATHERS: Do you think you can handle the work? I mean it's hard physical labor.

PAT: Well, sir, I was lucky there. They got me started on an exercise program at the treatment center and I have been keeping it up ever since. Besides, I've been putting in a full day's work on those temporary jobs. You can see by my job application. I've done lots of hard work.

MR. SMATHERS: You know, Sweeney, if you worked for us, the other workers might find out about this drug thing. Do you think you could handle that?

PAT: Yes, sir. I can handle it. That's one of the things we learned in the half-way house. How to get along with people when we were out again. You won't find me getting into trouble with the others. You won't have any problems with me.

MR. SMATHERS: I'll have to think about this, Sweeney. And I'll have to talk to the owner. Do you have any questions about the job?

PAT: No, sir. I think I understand what the job is about. And my only question would be when I could start. I would be willing to start as a temporary, or any other way you like.

MR. SMATHERS: Good. Then you will be hearing from us one way or another.

PAT: Thank you Mr. Smathers. Thank you for letting me tell my whole story. If you can see your way clear to hiring me, you will never be sorry. Good-bye.

MR. SMATHERS: Good-bye, Mr. Sweeney.

What Do You Think?

Rating the Applicant

A. Use the form below to show the kind of first impression Pat made on you. See page 16 for directions.

```
┌─────────────────────────────────────────────┐
│          First Impressions                   │
│                                              │
│ Scoring  Excellent......15  Fair........5    │
│          Good.........10    Poor........0    │
```

Item	Score
Grooming	
Clothing	
Posture/Body Control	
Eye Contact	
Manners	
Language	
Personality	
Total	

Rating ☐ Excellent 91–105 ☐ Fair . . 31–65
☐ Good . . . . 66–90 ☐ Poor . . 0–30

B. Rate Pat on each item below. Be ready to explain your rating.
1. **Preparation** (Was Pat well prepared for the interview?)
   ☐ Excellent   ☐ Fair
   ☐ Good   ☐ Poor
2. **Attitude** (Does Pat seem mostly positive or negative about himself, his previous jobs, and the new job?)
   ☐ Excellent   ☐ Fair
   ☐ Good   ☐ Poor
3. **Motivation** (Does Pat seem to really want the job?)
   ☐ Excellent   ☐ Fair
   ☐ Good   ☐ Poor
4. **Qualifications** (Does Pat seem to have the abilities and experience to do well on the job?)
   ☐ Excellent   ☐ Fair
   ☐ Good   ☐ Poor

Rating, *Continued*

5. **Listening/Answering/Asking** (Does Pat listen carefully, answer all questions fully, and ask important questions?)
   ☐ Excellent   ☐ Fair
   ☐ Good   ☐ Poor

Close-up on the Interview

A. Circle the words that best complete each sentence.
1. Pat wrote "to be explained..." on his job application in the box about
   a. convictions
   b. work history
   c. references
2. Pat figures he might have a chance at a job if he can just tell his story
   a. to his counselor
   b. to an interviewer
   c. to the workers
3. Pat makes a good case for himself by
   a. telling lies about his past
   b. giving good references
   c. speaking very positively about himself and his past work
4. Pat shows himself to be reasonable by offering
   a. to work for lower pay
   b. to take a part-time or temporary job
   c. to work a night shift

B. If you were Mr. Smathers, would you hire Pat?
☐ Yes   ☐ No   Why or why not?

_____

_____

_____

C. Do you think Pat closed the interview well?
☐ Yes   ☐ No   Why or why not?

_____

_____

_____

Bonus

Suppose an interviewer asked you why he or she should hire you instead of someone else. What would you say?

Potter's Apprentice

The Job

A potter's apprentice may:
- aid the potter in his or her work while learning to make pottery (ceramic) products
- follow the potter's directions in finishing parts of jobs, such as painting or kilning
- keep the studio clean and supplied with necessary materials
- pack and deliver products
- run errands

The Applicant

Phil Nowalski didn't do well in his high school subjects, except for art and shop. He liked to make things with his hands. None of the other subjects interested him very much.

Once out of high school, Phil tried several jobs—shipping clerk, factory worker, door-to-door salesman. None of these jobs made him happy.

Phil is now a driver for a wholesaler of gift items. He picks up products from factories and artists. And he delivers things to stores. He does not like this job much better than the others.

Today, Phil is picking up an order from a man who makes pottery products called *ceramics*. The potter makes vases, bowls, and other things out of clay.

Phil worked with clay himself when he was in school. He remembers that well, because he liked it. Everyone had said that the ceramics Phil made were really quite good.

When Phil arrives at the potter's studio, the potter is busy. He is shaping a bowl on the potter's wheel. Phil is watching the potter work.

Phil and Mr. King

PHIL: We didn't have one of those things in high school. We just shaped the clay with our hands and a cutting tool.

MR. KING: This is a potter's wheel. It's quite a trick to learn how to use it.

PHIL: I wish I could work like this. I like to make things.

MR. KING: Do you make things at home in your free time?

PHIL: No, I'm too tired by the time I get home. I usually just watch television.

MR. KING: Well, if you like to make things, you should do it. You don't have to buy a lot of equipment, you know. Here, hold this a minute, will you? (He gives Phil a bowl to hold. He puts the other things on shelves.) I'll take it now. I'm going to paint it. Then I'll put it in the kiln.

PHIL: We had a kiln at school. But the teacher never let us use it. She was the only one who could put things in the kiln. (He watches the potter paint a bowl.) What is that you're putting on the bowl?

MR. KING. This will give the bowl a red color.

PHIL: Oh yeah. Like all those bowls and vases you have over there. How come you're doing everything the same color?

MR. KING: That's what my customers like right now. I guess you might say it's becoming my style....Perhaps I should do something different. Use another color. (He takes a painted bowl to the kiln.) Don't get too close. It's real hot.

PHIL: How many bowls can you do at a time in this kiln? It looks bigger than the one at school.

MR. KING: Let's see. It handles about four of these bowls. It all depends on what you're making. (He finishes loading the kiln.) Now I can take care of that order for your boss. Want to give me a hand?

PHIL: Sure! Just show me what you want me to do. (Both men pack boxes. They continue to talk.) You do all the work here yourself? Don't you need any help?

MR. KING: Well, I have been doing it all myself. But things are getting to be a little too much for me now. Business is building up. And I'm falling behind. I was here late last night finishing up this order for your boss.

PHIL: Yeah, you sure could use some help. You know, I would like to learn this work. I never have been able to find any kind of job I liked. But I know I would like this, making things with my own hands.

MR. KING: Wait a minute! I don't even know your name.

PHIL: It's Phil. Phil Nowalski. Say, why don't you hire me to be your apprentice? I'll help you with all of the jobs around here. And you could be training me to be a potter. How about it?

MR. KING: It's something to think about. Did you graduate from high school?

PHIL: Yes, two years ago.

MR. KING: What kind of work have you done since then?

PHIL: I've had lots of jobs. But they have all been lousy. I've never had a job where I could learn something I was really interested in.

MR. KING: What makes you think I could teach you? Or that you would be able to learn?

PHIL: I could show you the things I made in art classes at school. And I just know I could learn from you. The things you make are beautiful!

MR. KING: Well, Phil, a little flattery never hurts....Let's get these boxes on your truck and then we can talk some more about it.

What Do You Think?

Rating the Applicant

Since Phil's talk with Mr. King is not like a regular job interview, *Grooming* and *Clothing* have been dropped from the rating form. *Preparation* has been dropped from the ratings in Part B.

A. Use the form below to show the kind of first impression Phil made on you. See page 16 for directions.

See page 16 for directions.

First Impressions

Scoring   Excellent.......15   Fair.........5
           Good 10   Poor.........0

Item	Score
Posture/Body Control	
Eye Contact	
Manners	
Language	
Personality	
Total	

Rating   ☐ Excellent   61–75   ☐ Fair . . 21–40
         ☐ Good 41–60   ☐ Poor . . 0–20

B. Rate Phil on each item below. Be ready to explain your rating.

1. **Attitude** (Does Phil seem mostly positive or negative about himself, his previous jobs, and the new job?)
   ☐ Excellent   ☐ Fair
   ☐ Good   ☐ Poor

2. **Motivation** (Does Phil seem to really want to work for Mr. King?)
   ☐ Excellent   ☐ Fair
   ☐ Good   ☐ Poor

3. **Qualifications** (Does Phil seem to have the abilities and experience to do well on the job?)
   ☐ Excellent   ☐ Fair
   ☐ Good   ☐ Poor

Rating, *Continued*

4. **Listening/Answering/Asking** (Does Phil listen carefully, answer all questions fully, and ask important questions?)
   ☐ Excellent   ☐ Fair
   ☐ Good   ☐ Poor

Close-up on the Interview

A. Write **T** if the statement is true. Write **F** if it is false. Be ready to explain your answer.

___ 1. Phil is unhappy with his job because it doesn't give him a chance to do things he likes to do.

___ 2. Phil should have thought about the kinds of things he likes to do before he started looking for jobs.

___ 3. One good thing about the driving job is it gives Phil a chance to see many different work places.

___ 4. At first, Phil didn't realize that he might be able to get a job helping Mr. King.

B. If you were Mr. King, would you hire Phil?
☐ Yes   ☐ No   Why or why not?

_____

_____

_____

_____

_____

C. If you could talk to Phil, what advice would you give him?

_____

_____

_____

_____

_____

Bonus

Suppose an interviewer asked you to tell about your interests and the kinds of things you do in your spare time? What would you say?

Forestry Worker

The Job

A forestry worker may:

- help to prevent and control forest fires and erosion
- help build fire roads
- plant new trees
- take part in logging by marking trees to be cut, cutting them down, and clearing away logs
- clean and service picnic and camping areas open to the public

The Applicant

Henry Allcot spent three years in a state camp for boys. He went in at 15 for stealing cars. Henry finished high school in the camp. He also learned a lot about forestry.

Back in River City, Henry was worried. In two months, he had not been able to get a job. He had to explain where he had spent his time. Interviewers said they would consider him, but no one hired him.

Henry talked to a counselor at the State Employment Office. He told the counselor, "I was a lot better off at the camp. You know, I liked working in the forest."

The counselor looked at Henry. "If you liked it, why don't you make it your career?" he asked.

Henry thought about this. It made sense. The counselor gave him a list of names and addresses. His list covered federal and state agencies and private companies.

Henry decided to try the private companies first. He sent each of them a letter. He told them he was looking for a job in forestry. He told them what his experience was, and where he got it.

Henry got answers to every letter. He liked the letter from Timberwood Forest Management Company best. He is now being interviewed by the manager of Timberwood, Mr. Kurt Jurgenson. He has appointments for other interviews after this one.

Henry and Mr. Jurgenson

Directions

- Use the photos to rate Henry's grooming, clothing, posture, body control, and eye contact.
- As you read the interview, note Henry's manners, language, personality, preparation, attitude, motivation, and qualifications. Also note the way he listens, the answers he gives, and the questions he asks.
- Underline any of Henry's statements that may help him get the job. Circle any of Henry's statements that may hurt his chances. Box any statements that may not be harmful but could be improved.

MR. JURGENSON: You couldn't have picked a nicer day to come up to the mountains, Henry.

HENRY: Yes, sir. It's just like I remember it to be. I love it up here. (He laughs.) Even better now, because I can come and go as I please.

MR. JURGENSON: Yes, I suppose that does make it very different. I sort of felt that way myself once, when I was in the army. You know, I'm from the city too. It was when I was in the army that I got to know this country around here.

HENRY: Is that right? I didn't know there was an army camp around here.

MR. JURGENSON: It's the State Camp for Boys now. You might say we have been to the same school.

HENRY: How about that! (He laughs.) The same school! Yeah, now I remember. Someone said it used to be an army camp. Did they have you guys fighting fires too?

MR. JURGENSON: Among other things. We didn't get much time off either. But then I don't think we had it as bad as you.

HENRY: Oh, it was not so bad, Mr. Jurgenson. It could have been a whole lot worse for doing what I did to get sent there. Stealing cars I mean.

MR. JURGENSON: Lots of boys get in trouble, Henry...Would you like a cup of coffee?

HENRY: Oh, uh...no thank you, sir. I've been drinking coffee all the way up here.

MR. JURGENSON: Tell me what you know about forestry, Henry. Which jobs did you like doing the most?

HENRY: What we did at the camp was mostly conservation things. We marked trees for cutting, trees that were sick or needed thinning out. We cut down those trees and then cut them into logs. Then we would pull the logs out of the forest. A lot of the time we cleared away the brush to help prevent fires. And made fire roads. Then, as you know, we helped put out forest fires.

MR. JURGENSON: Yes, I know. Our men worked on many of the same fires as the boys from the camp. As a matter of fact, we have men working for us now who have spent time at the camp.

HENRY: Is that right? I wonder if any of the guys who were in with me are here now. Who do you have here?

MR. JURGENSON: We can go into that later, Henry. Tell me more about your work experience.

HENRY: Oh, all right…We would clean up after the fire too. Oh, yeah, and we would plant new trees. I think I liked that best of all. We would go into places where the trees had been cut down or where there had been a fire and we would plant little trees.

MR. JURGENSON: Just what kind of life do you expect to lead up here, Henry?

HENRY: Sir, I want to learn more about forestry. Some day maybe I can get to be a forestry aid. I would like to have a family of my own too. I could teach my kids all about the forest.

MR. JURGENSON: Henry, why don't you stay here with us for a day or so. It will give you a chance to meet the men and see what the place is like. How about it?

HENRY: Thanks, Mr. Jurgenson. Trouble is, I have another interview this afternoon…Then, later on, I've got to get over to the State Camp. I wrote and told some of my old friends that I would come and visit them today.

MR. JURGENSON: All right, Henry. I don't want to change your plans. If you have other people to see…

What Do You Think?

Rating the Applicant

A. Use the form below to show the kind of first impression Henry made on you. See page 16 for directions.

First Impressions

Scoring   Excellent 15   Fair 5
               Good 10   Poor 0

Item	Score
Grooming	
Clothing	
Posture/Body Control	
Eye Contact	
Manners	
Language	
Personality	
Total	

Rating   ☐ Excellent 91–105   ☐ Fair . . 31–65
              ☐ Good 66–90   ☐ Poor . . 0–30

B. Rate Henry on each item below. Be ready to explain your rating.

1. **Preparation** (Was Henry well prepared for the interview?)
   ☐ Excellent   ☐ Fair
   ☐ Good   ☐ Poor
2. **Attitude** (Does Henry seem mostly positive or negative about himself, his previous experience, and the new job?)
   ☐ Excellent   ☐ Fair
   ☐ Good   ☐ Poor
3. **Motivation** (Does Henry seem to really want the job?)
   ☐ Excellent   ☐ Fair
   ☐ Good   ☐ Poor
4. **Qualifications** (Does Henry seem to have the abilities and experience to do well on the job?)
   ☐ Excellent   ☐ Fair
   ☐ Good   ☐ Poor

Rating, *Continued*

5. **Listening/Answering/Asking** (Does Henry listen carefully, answer all questions fully, and ask important questions?)
   ☐ Excellent   ☐ Fair
   ☐ Good   ☐ Poor

Close-up on the Interview

A. Fill in the word that best completes each sentence.

     experience   reasonable
     questions   time

1. Henry showed that he would be a good forestry worker by telling a lot about his previous work _____.
2. Henry should have allowed more _____ for the interview.
3. He also should have asked more _____ about the job Mr. Jurgenson had in mind.
4. Henry would have seemed more _____ to Mr. Jurgenson if he had offered to change his plans.

B. If you were Mr. Jurgenson, would you hire Henry? ☐ Yes   ☐ No   Why or why not?

_____

_____

_____

_____

_____

C. If you could talk to Henry, what advice would you give him?

_____

_____

_____

_____

Bonus

Suppose an interviewer asked you to tell about the kind of work you would like to be doing three years from now. What would you say?

Retail Sales Worker

The Job

A retail sales worker may:

- make out sales checks, receive cash and credit-card payments, and give change and receipts
- use point-of-sale computer terminals that register sales, adjust inventory figures, and perform calculations
- wrap purchases
- handle returns and exchanges of merchandise
- keep work area neat
- help stock shelves and racks, mark price tags, take inventory, and prepare displays
- interest customers in merchandise for sale by describing how the product is made, demonstrating its use, showing various models and colors, and helping the customer make choices

The Applicant

Helen Chen has learned helpful job search and interview skills at the Job Search Center run by her state's employment department. Now she is trying to find a job selling women's clothing.

Helen made a list of good clothing stores. Then she went out to visit these stores. If the sales workers weren't too busy she asked them questions like these:

- How long has the store been in business?
- What kind of customer do they mostly sell to?
- What is the store's policy about how to treat customers?

- Do they know of any job openings?
- Whom should I contact about a job?

One sales worker admired the way Helen was going about finding a job. She offered to introduce Helen to the manager. Helen is now being interviewed by the manager, Mrs. Gordan.

Helen and Mrs. Gordan

Directions

- Use the photos to rate Helen's grooming, clothing, posture, body control, and eye contact.
- As you read the interview, note Helen's manners, language, personality, preparation, attitude, motivation, and qualifications. Also note the way she listens, the answers she gives, and the questions she asks.
- <u>Underline</u> any of Helen's statements that may help her get the job. (Circle) any of Helen's statements that may hurt her chances. [Box] any statements that may not be harmful but could be improved.

MRS. GORDAN: I understand you are looking for a job, Miss Chen.

HELEN: Yes, ma'am. I've always been interested in clothing and fashion. So I decided to look for a fashion sales job.

MRS. GORDAN: I see. And why do you think you might like to work here at Modern Fashions?

HELEN: Well, you seem to have beautiful clothes—things I would like to wear. So I think I would enjoy selling them to others. You carry brands that are advertised in fashion magazines. You have been in business a long time. Your sales people are very good with customers. I know I could learn a lot from them. Also, I...

MRS. GORDAN: Well, I'm very impressed, Miss Chen. You seem to have taken the trouble to find out something about us before asking for a job. You would be surprised how few people do that. But now I'd like to know something about you. How do you keep up on fashions?

HELEN: I go to the library and look through the fashion magazines at least once a month. I also visit the stores, even if I can't afford to buy anything.

MRS. GORDAN: I see. As you have noticed we give a lot of attention to our customers. Sometimes the customers are very demanding though. What makes you think you could handle them?

HELEN: Well, I'm sure I could learn a lot about that from your sales workers. But I do have experience working with all kinds of people. I have taken care of children. I have sold cookies and greeting cards from door to door in all kinds of neighborhoods. And I have done volunteer work for my community.

MRS. GORDAN: How well did you do with the sales of cookies and greeting cards?

HELEN: (smiling) Well, I sold every box of cookies or cards that I was given to sell.

MRS. GORDAN: Suppose I asked a close friend of yours what your best quality was. What do you think they would tell me?

HELEN: Hmm, that's a hard one. Let me see...I guess they would say my best quality is I'm good with people. I like to help them and I'm good at getting them to do things.

MRS. GORDAN: Are you planning to get married anytime soon, Miss Chen?

HELEN: Uh...I don't understand what that has to do with my ability to do the job.

MRS. GORDAN: Oh, it's just that if I find someone and train them, I don't like to lose them.

HELEN: Well, I don't think it is a fair question, Mrs. Gordan. Even if I got married I would continue working, because I want my own career.

MRS. GORDAN: Good enough, Miss Chen. I tell you, I am going to need someone this summer to fill in when people take their vacations. If you worked out well, perhaps I might consider keeping you on. We are going to be needing people for a branch store that's opening in the fall. Would you be interested?

HELEN: May I ask what the pay would be?

MRS. GORDAN: Of course. I would start you at four seventy five ($4.75) an hour. If you stayed on you would go on salary plus commission. Some of our top sales people earn more than eight dollars ($8.00) an hour that way. But it takes a few years to get up there. We also have a health plan for those who stay with us at least a year.

HELEN: That sounds great! Yes, I would be very interested, Mrs. Gordan.

What Do You Think?

Rating the Applicant

A. Use the form below to show the kind of first impression Helen made on you. See page 16 for directions.

First Impressions	
Scoring Excellent.......15 Fair........5 Good.........10 Poor........0	

Item	Score
Grooming	
Clothing	
Posture/Body Control	
Eye Contact	
Manners	
Language	
Personality	
Total	

Rating   ☐ Excellent 91–105   ☐ Fair . . 31–65
         ☐ Good 66–90   ☐ Poor . . 0–30

B. Rate Helen on each item below. Be ready to explain your rating.
1. **Preparation** (Was Helen well prepared for the interview?)
   ☐ Excellent   ☐ Fair
   ☐ Good   ☐ Poor
2. **Attitude** (Does Helen seem mostly positive or negative about herself, her previous jobs, and the new job?)
   ☐ Excellent   ☐ Fair
   ☐ Good   ☐ Poor
3. **Motivation** (Does Helen seem to really want the job?)
   ☐ Excellent   ☐ Fair
   ☐ Good   ☐ Poor
4. **Qualifications** (Does Helen seem to have the abilities and experience to do well on the job?)
   ☐ Excellent   ☐ Fair
   ☐ Good   ☐ Poor

Rating, *Continued*

5. **Listening/Answering/Asking** (Does Helen listen carefully, answer all questions fully, and ask important questions?)
   ☐ Excellent   ☐ Fair
   ☐ Good   ☐ Poor

Close-up on the Interview

A. Answer the questions below.
1. What is Helen doing in order to find the kind of job she would like?

   _____
   _____
   _____

2. What does she do to keep up on women's fashions?

   _____
   _____
   _____

3. What are some ways in which she shows Mrs. Gordan that she would be a good worker?

   _____
   _____
   _____

B. If you were Mrs. Gordan, would you hire Helen? ☐ Yes   ☐ No   Why or why not?

   _____
   _____
   _____

C. Do you think Helen closes the interview well? ☐ Yes   ☐ No   Why or why not?

   _____
   _____
   _____

Bonus

Suppose an interviewer asked you to tell what you think your best quality is. What would you say?

Hotel Bellhop

The Job

A hotel bellhop may:

- show hotel guests to their rooms, carrying their baggage by hand or on a hand truck
- explain how to use the television set, temperature controls, and telephone
- check the room for supplies
- carry out baggage when guests are leaving
- page guests in public rooms
- deliver messages and run errands
- deliver laundry, dry cleaning, and food and drinks
- keep lobby clean

The Applicant

Jack Birdsong got the idea of working in a hotel while he was watching an old movie on television. He thought he would like hotel work because it involved meeting many different kinds of people. It must be exciting, he thought, people coming and going all the time.

The next day Jack went to the State Job Search Center in River City. A counselor there gave him a little book that described all the things hotel workers do.

Jack read the book carefully. He decided that almost any job in a hotel would suit him. But if he could, he would like to be a bellhop. That way, he could meet new guests. And he liked the idea of tips and wearing a uniform, too. "It's a good career field," he thought.

"There will always be hotel jobs in River City."

The counselor told Jack to call some hotels and try to get an interview. Jack got appointments at three of River City's hotels. He is now about to be interviewed at the Ritz-Ambassador Hotel by Mr. Schmidt, the personnel manager. A few friends are with him.

Jack and Mr. Schmidt

Directions

- Use the photos to rate Jack's grooming, clothing, posture, body control, and eye contact.
- As you read the interview, note Jack's manners, language, personality, preparation, attitude, motivation, and qualifications. Also note the way he listens, the answers he gives, and the questions he asks.
- <u>Underline</u> any of Jack's statements that may help him get the job. Circle any of Jack's statements that may hurt his chances. Box any statements that may not be harmful but could be improved.

MR. SCHMIDT: Are you all here to see about working at the hotel?

JACK: No, Mr. Schmidt. Just me. These are my friends. We are going to the movies later.

MR. SCHMIDT: Then you are the young man who called me about a bellhop job.

JACK: That's right, sir. I'm Jack Birdsong.

MR. SCHMIDT: All right. Why don't you other guys wait for your friend in the lobby. He won't be very long. (Mr. Schmidt takes Jack to his office. They both sit down.)

JACK: This is a really big place, this hotel. It's bigger than I thought it would be.

MR. SCHMIDT: It is the largest hotel in River City. Let me look at your application here...I see you're over 18. You graduated from Franklin High School. Do you have a Social Security card?

JACK: Yes I do, Mr. Schmidt. But I forgot to bring it, and I couldn't remember the number so I left that space blank. By the way, I have a driver's license too. I have that with me if you'd like to see it.

MR. SCHMIDT: No, that's all right. Why don't you tell me something about yourself?

JACK: All right. Let's see, you know I graduated from Franklin High. I was in the school marching band. I carried the state flag in the color guard. And I was on the wrestling team too.

MR. SCHMIDT: The wrestling team? I used to wrestle myself. What class were you in, 120-pound?

66

JACK: That's right! I started out at 100. But I grew a lot when I was 16. What class did you wrestle in?

MR. SCHMIDT: I was in the 145-pound class at State. But I wrestled in your weight for a while in high school.... Jack, have you ever had a job before?

JACK: No, sir. I've tried to find part-time jobs and summer jobs. But I could never get one. There were always so many kids in River City looking for jobs. Oh—I have helped out in my aunt's store from time to time. She has a little neighborhood food store.

MRS. SCHMIDT: What do you know about hotel work, Jack?

JACK: I only know about it from books really. And from what I've seen in movies and on TV.

MR. SCHMIDT: From what you saw on the way in, do you think you would like working in a big hotel like this?

JACK: Yes, I think so, Mr. Schmidt. There seems to be a lot going on.

MR. SCHMIDT: There usually is. But we have an even heavier schedule this week. There's a state-wide teachers' conference going on. How would you say that you get along with people, Jack?

JACK: Oh, pretty good, I think. I never had any trouble at school much.... Oh sometimes I got bothered when someone made a silly Indian joke. Calling me Chief or Crazy Horse or something. But I get along all right.

MR. SCHMIDT: And you would like to be a bellhop. Is that right?

JACK: Yes, sir. I think I would like that best. But I wouldn't mind some of the other jobs either. I mean, I just think I would be better as a bellhop. Are the bellhops the guys in the green uniforms near the front door?

MR. SCHMIDT: Some of them are bellhops. The fellows in the short jackets. There are also parking attendants. Do you think you could be a parking attendant, Jack?

JACK: Well...yes. I could do that....I never thought about it before.

MR. SCHMIDT: Good. Now let me tell you about the things we look for in employees of the Ritz-Ambassador.

What Do You Think?

Rating the Applicant

A. Use the form below to show the kind of first impression Jack made on you. See page 16 for directions.

```
┌─────────────────────────────────────────┐
│           First Impressions              │
│  Scoring  Excellent.......15  Fair.......5│
│           Good .........10  Poor........0 │
├──────────────────────────┬──────────────┤
│          Item            │    Score     │
├──────────────────────────┼──────────────┤
│  Grooming                │              │
├──────────────────────────┼──────────────┤
│  Clothing                │              │
├──────────────────────────┼──────────────┤
│  Posture/Body Control    │              │
├──────────────────────────┼──────────────┤
│  Eye Contact             │              │
├──────────────────────────┼──────────────┤
│  Manners                 │              │
├──────────────────────────┼──────────────┤
│  Language                │              │
├──────────────────────────┼──────────────┤
│  Personality             │              │
├──────────────────────────┼──────────────┤
│              Total       │              │
└──────────────────────────┴──────────────┘
  Rating  ☐ Excellent 91–105   ☐ Fair . . 31–65
          ☐ Good . . . . 66–90  ☐ Poor . . 0–30
```

B. Rate Jack on each item below. Be ready to explain your rating.
1. **Preparation** (Was Jack well prepared for the interview?)
   ☐ Excellent   ☐ Fair
   ☐ Good   ☐ Poor
2. **Attitude** (Does Jack seem mostly positive or negative about himself, his previous jobs, and the new job?)
   ☐ Excellent   ☐ Fair
   ☐ Good   ☐ Poor
3. **Motivation** (Does Jack seem to really want the job?)
   ☐ Excellent   ☐ Fair
   ☐ Good   ☐ Poor
4. **Qualifications** (Does Jack seem to have the abilities and experience to do well on the job?)
   ☐ Excellent   ☐ Fair
   ☐ Good   ☐ Poor

Rating, *Continued*

5. **Listening/Answering/Asking** (Does Jack listen carefully, answer all questions fully, and ask important questions?)
   ☐ Excellent   ☐ Fair
   ☐ Good   ☐ Poor

Close-up on the Interview

A. Answer the questions below.
1. Do you think Jack seems grown up?
   ☐ Yes   ☐ No   Why or why not?

   _____

   _____

2. What could Jack have done to better prepare for the interview?

   _____

   _____

3. Why might it be a good idea to tell an interviewer about the extra things you did at school—such as being on a team or belonging to a club?

   _____

   _____

B. If you were Mr. Schmidt, would you hire Jack?
   ☐ Yes   ☐ No   Why or why not?

   _____

   _____

   _____

C. If you could talk to Jack, what advice would you give him?

   _____

   _____

   _____

Bonus

Suppose an interviewer asked you to tell about any of the extra things you did at school. What would you say?

interview 14

Delivery Driver

The Job

A delivery driver may:

- drive vans, pickup trucks, or light trucks
- be dispatched by radio or telephone
- pick up and deliver packages
- write receipts for goods picked up
- collect money
- inspect vehicle for gas, oil, water, tire pressure and proper operation of brakes
- perform emergency roadside repairs such as changing tires and installing tire chains

The Applicant

Dianne Low-Quan loves to drive. She would like to drive vans and trucks. Now that she has become 21 years old she can apply for a job as a delivery driver. Because of insurance requirements, no one in River City would hire her as a driver until she turned 21.

The week of her birthday, Dianne looked in the newspaper help wanted ads for driver jobs. This ad caught her eye.

> • **DRIVERS** •
>
> Rapid Express is looking for full-time drivers. Must be 21 yrs old. Apply in person with DMV printout not more than 10 days old. 657 85th Ave. 9–5 Mon. thru Fri.

Dianne drove down to the nearest office of the Department of Motor Vehicles and got a computer printout of her driving record. The printout shows any moving violations she has been stopped for during the last three years and any serious accidents she has had.

Dianne drove over to the address in the ad. The receptionist gave her an application to fill out. Soon Dianne was called in to see the interviewer, Ms. Lupo.

Dianne and Ms. Lupo

<table>
<tr><td valign="top" width="45%">

Directions

- Use the photos to rate Dianne's grooming, clothing, posture, body control, and eye contact.
- As you read the interview, note Dianne's manners, language, personality, preparation, attitude, motivation, and qualifications. Also note the way she listens, the answers she gives, and the questions she asks.
- <u>Underline</u> any of Dianne's statements that may help her get the job. (Circle) any of Dianne's statements that may hurt her chances. [Box] any statements that may not be harmful but could be improved.

</td><td valign="top">

MS. LUPO: Have a seat please.

DIANNE: Thank you.

MS. LUPO: Why do you want to be a driver, Ms. Low-Quan?

DIANNE: Well...uh...I like to drive.

MS. LUPO: Any other reason?

DIANNE: Yes, well you're on your own... and you're not cooped up inside all day.

MS. LUPO: (She looks at Dianne's DMV printout.) Looks like you have a pretty clean driving record. Only one speeding ticket. How did you get that?

DIANNE: I didn't see the cop until it was too late.

MS. LUPO: (She laughs.) I see. How would you describe yourself as a driver, Ms. Low-Quan?

DIANNE: What do you mean?

MS. LUPO: I mean would a passenger feel comfortable riding with you or would they feel their life was at risk?

DIANNE: Oh, I drive OK. I'm pretty careful. I've never had any accidents.

MS. LUPO: How well do you know the city? Are you familiar with most of the neighborhoods?

DIANNE: Yeah. My father said that would be important if I wanted a job as a driver. So I've been driving around different parts of the city every weekend. I think I know it pretty well now.

MS. LUPO: Can you read a road map?

DIANNE: Sure.

MS. LUPO: OK. Well, we have a little test I would like you to take now. I'm going to give you a map of the city and some addresses. I would like you to use the

</td></tr>
</table>

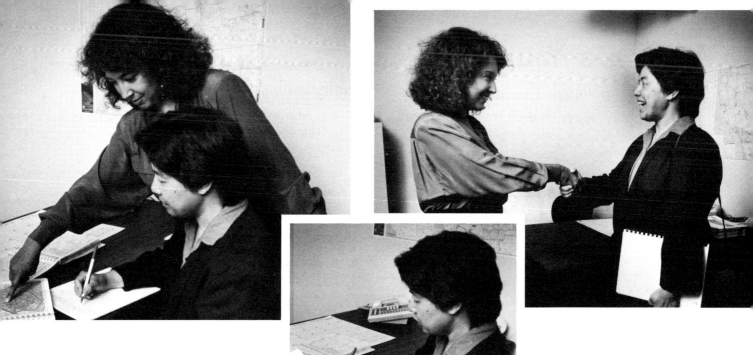

map to tell how you would get from one address to another. You will have 15 minutes to finish the test. Then we'll talk some more.

Dianne finishes the test and Ms. Lupo quickly scores it.

MS. LUPO: Well, Ms. Low-Quan. It looks like you should have no trouble getting around the city. Let me ask you, why would you like to work for Rapid Express?

DIANNE: I always see your vans out on the streets. I see your drivers running in and out of offices and stores. It looks like they are doing important work. I knew a long time ago that I wanted to be a driver too, but I had to wait until I became 21.

MS. LUPO: And can you move quickly?

DIANNE: Yes, ma'am. When there's a good enough reason for me to do it.

MS. LUPO: Let me tell you about the job. The way we get business is by being faster than other delivery services. So you have to move fast. But you also have to obey the traffic laws. You have to drive smart and walk fast. The starting pay is five fifty ($5.50) an hour. We have some benefits you can read about on this sheet. (She hands Dianne a sheet of paper.) Are you interested?

DIANNE: Yes.

MS. LUPO: OK. We'll have to check out your references. Is it OK if we call your present employer?

DIANNE: Yes, they know I'm looking for a driving job.

MS. LUPO: Good. Any questions?

DIANNE: How soon will you let me know if I get the job?

MS. LUPO: Early next week.

DIANNE: I hope I get it. I've been waiting for three years.

MS. LUPO: Your chances are very good, Ms. Low-Quan, so long as your references check out OK.

DIANNE: Thanks for telling me. Good-bye.

MS. LUPO: Bye.

What Do You Think?

Rating the Applicant

A. Use the form below to show the kind of first impression Dianne made on you. See page 16 for directions.

┌───┐
| **First Impressions** |
| |
| **Scoring** Excellent......15 Fair........5 |
| Good.........10 Poor........0 |

Item	Score
Grooming	
Clothing	
Posture/Body Control	
Eye Contact	
Manners	
Language	
Personality	
Total	

Rating   ☐ Excellent 91–105   ☐ Fair . .31–65
             ☐ Good 66–90   ☐ Poor . .0–30

└───┘

B. Rate Dianne on each item below. Be ready to explain your rating.
1. **Preparation** (Was Dianne well prepared for the interview?)
   ☐ Excellent   ☐ Fair
   ☐ Good   ☐ Poor
2. **Attitude** (Does Dianne seem mostly positive or negative about herself, her previous jobs, and the new job?)
   ☐ Excellent   ☐ Fair
   ☐ Good   ☐ Poor
3. **Motivation** (Does Dianne seem to really want the job?)
   ☐ Excellent   ☐ Fair
   ☐ Good   ☐ Poor
4. **Qualifications** (Does Dianne seem to have the abilities and experience to do well on the job?)
   ☐ Excellent   ☐ Fair
   ☐ Good   ☐ Poor

Rating, *Continued*

5. **Listening/Answering/Asking** (Does Dianne listen carefully, answer all questions fully, and ask important questions?)
   ☐ Excellent   ☐ Fair
   ☐ Good   ☐ Poor

Close-up on the Interview

A. Answer the questions below.
1. How did Dianne prepare herself for getting a job as a delivery driver?

   _____

   _____

2. Do you think Dianne closed the interview well? ☐ Yes   ☐ No   ☐ Why or why not?

   _____

   _____

3. Why do you think you have to be a certain age and have a good driving record to get a job as a driver?

   _____

   _____

B. If you were Ms. Lupo, would you hire Dianne?
   ☐ Yes   ☐ No   Why or why not?

   _____

   _____

   _____

C. If you could talk to Dianne, what advice would you give her?

   _____

   _____

Bonus

Suppose an interviewer asked you the questions below. What would you say?
1. Can you read a road map?
2. How well do you know your way around town?
3. How is your driving record?

Janitor

The Job

A janitor may:
- keep office buildings, hospitals, stores, apartment houses, and other types of buildings clean and in good condition
- mop and wax floors, vacuum carpets, dust furniture, empty trash baskets
- wash windows
- clean bathrooms
- replenish bathroom supplies
- fix leaky faucets and make other minor repairs
- do painting and minor carpentry
- see that heating and air conditioning are properly set
- mow lawns, trim shrubbery
- exterminate insects and rodents

The Applicant

Mike Graziano was just finishing school and he needed to get a job. His uncle suggested that he try to find work as a janitor. He said that with all the office buildings in River City, there would always be a need for janitorial services. He said that someday Mike could probably own his own janitorial service company.

Mike liked that idea about someday owning his own company. He wanted to become a boss as soon as possible.

Mike got out the telephone book and turned to the yellow pages. He looked for this listing: **Janitor Service**. He found dozens of companies listed. Many of them had ads that told about the kinds of services the companies provided.

Mike called 10 of the companies that looked good to him. All offered to send him a job application that he could fill out and return by mail. They would then notify him when they had an opening.

Mike filled out and returned each application. He soon had an appointment for an interview with Mr. Arthur Diaz at the D & L Janitorial Service. The interview is now in progress.

Mike and Mr. Diaz

Directions

- Use the photos to rate Mike's grooming, clothing, posture, body control, and eye contact.
- As you read the interview, note Mike's manners, language, personality, preparation, attitude, motivation, and qualifications. Also note the way he listens, the answers he gives, and the questions he asks.
- Underline any of Mike's statements that may help him get the job. Circle any of Mike's statements that may hurt his chances. Box any statements that may not be harmful but could be improved.

MR. DIAZ: Do you know what a janitor does?

MIKE: Oh sure, Art. I've seen the janitors at work in school. Looks real easy. Say, how long do you have to be with the company before you can become a supervisor?

MR. DIAZ: That depends on the person and on when we have openings.

MIKE: I want to become a supervisor soon as I can. Then someday I want to start my own business.

MR. DIAZ: You don't say. Well it's OK to be ambitious, but first you need to get some experience. There's a lot more to learn about janitorial work than you may think.

MIKE: What is there to learn?

MR. DIAZ: How to mop and wax floors for hours without tiring yourself out. How to get stubborn stains out of rugs. What kinds of cleansers, waxes, and polishes to use for different kinds of floors and furniture. How to make minor repairs. And lots more.

MIKE: I see what you mean, Art. But I think I could learn that stuff pretty fast.

MR. DIAZ: What makes you think so?

MIKE: Well, I always pick up pretty quick on how to fix things and keep them looking pretty good. Like my car, for instance. It's 10 years old but looks like new. I'm always washing and waxing it.

MR. DIAZ: I see. And what else can you tell me about yourself?

MIKE: Well, let's see. I live with my mother and stepfather. But I want to get a place of my own as soon as I save some money. You know how it goes, Art, living at home.

MR. DIAZ: Mike, what could you tell me that would make me believe you would be a good worker?

MIKE: Well, Art, I'm just a great person! Ask anybody! (He sees that Mr. Diaz is not amused.) Sorry, Art, I was just joking. But you could ask Mr. Ferris. I wrote him down on the application there. Ferris Hauling Company. I help him out sometimes. He's always telling people what a good worker I am.

MR. DIAZ: How come you aren't going to work for him after you get out of school?

MIKE: No future there, Art. He can't afford to pay much and he's going to retire soon anyway. By the way, how much does this job pay? I have to make at least four fifty ($4.50) an hour to make it. I figured that out.

MR. DIAZ: This position starts at five dollars ($5.00) an hour.

MIKE: Hey, that's even better. How about overtime? You pay time-and-a-half?

MR. DIAZ: Yes, there is time-and-a-half for overtime. And we have employer-paid health insurance.

MIKE: Sounds real good, Art. What are the hours? I would like to work at night if I could. That way I don't have to run into my stepfather that much. (He laughs.) If you know what I mean.

MR. DIAZ: Well, most of our work is done after businesses close for the day…Mike, I see from your application here that you have no convictions. Do you know any reason why you couldn't be bonded?

MIKE: Bonded? What's that?

MR. DIAZ: It's like insurance. If any of our employees steal something from a place where they are working, the bonding company pays the loss.

MIKE: Hey, I never stole anything in my life! And I've never had any trouble with the cops! What do you take me for?

MR. DIAZ: We have to ask everyone about that, Mike. Don't take it personally. If you want to work in this business, you have to be bondable.

MIKE: Sorry, Art. I guess you're right. I do have a lot to learn about this business.

MR. DIAZ: Mike, I'm glad you realize you have a lot to learn. But now tell me this: Why should I believe that you would be a good janitor?

MIKE: Well, I…

What Do You Think?

Rating the Applicant

A. Use the form below to show the kind of first impression Mike made on you. See page 16 for directions.

First Impressions

Scoring Excellent.......15 Fair 5
Good ....10 Poor........0

Item	Score
Grooming	
Clothing	
Posture/Body Control	
Eye Contact	
Manners	
Language	
Personality	
Total	

Rating ☐ Excellent 91–105 ☐ Fair . .31–65
☐ Good ....66–90 ☐ Poor ..0–30

B. Rate Mike on each item below. Be ready to explain your rating.
1. **Preparation** (Was Mike well prepared for the interview?)
   ☐ Excellent ☐ Fair
   ☐ Good ☐ Poor
2. **Attitude** (Does Mike seem mostly positive or negative about himself, his previous jobs, and the new job?)
   ☐ Excellent ☐ Fair
   ☐ Good ☐ Poor
3. **Motivation** (Does Mike seem to really want the job?)
   ☐ Excellent ☐ Fair
   ☐ Good ☐ Poor
4. **Qualifications** (Does Mike seem to have the abilities and experience to do well on the job?)
   ☐ Excellent ☐ Fair
   ☐ Good ☐ Poor

Rating, *Continued*

5. **Listening/Answering/Asking** (Does Mike listen carefully, answer all questions fully, and ask important questions?)
   ☐ Excellent ☐ Fair
   ☐ Good ☐ Poor

Close-up on the Interview

A. Answer the questions below.
1. In what way does Mike show poor interview manners?

   _____

   _____

   _____

2. How do Mike's feelings about what he needs to learn change during the interview?

   _____

   _____

   _____

3. What could Mike say to convince Mr. Diaz that he really would be a good janitor?

   _____

   _____

   _____

B. If you were Mr. Diaz, would you hire Mike?
   ☐ Yes ☐ No Why or why not?

   _____

   _____

   _____

C. If you could talk to Mike, what advice would you give him?

   _____

   _____

   _____

Bonus

Suppose an interviewer asked you to tell why he or she should believe that you would be a good worker. What would you say?

Your Interview Skills Test

By reading the Guidelines for Job Applicants and by rating and discussing the interviews in this book, you have learned many things you should and should not do on job interviews. Now you can apply what you have learned.

As the next step in developing your interview skills, you are going to be interviewed for a job yourself. The job is with MaryAnn's, a chain of fast food restaurants.

E. Tong

The Place of Employment

The photo above shows a new MaryAnn's fast food restaurant. This new MaryAnn's is open from 7:00 in the morning until midnight. But some of the 11 MaryAnn's restaurants in your area are open 24 hours a day. All these opened in the last five years. Most of the employees work full time. But there are also some part-time employees.

MaryAnn's is looking for people to work as counter workers and cooks in the new restaurant. This is the ad that they placed in the help-wanted section of your newspaper.

Paste
your
picture
here.

OPPORTUNITY KNOCKS!

Here is your chance to join America's fastest-growing restaurant company. We want hard-working men and women 18 or over to grow with us! Now hiring for positions as counter workers and cooks at the newest MaryAnn's restaurant. No experience necessary. Write and tell us about yourself.

MaryAnn's Restaurants, P.O. Box 1111
An Equal Opportunity Employer

You have answered the ad with a letter, saying you would like a chance to grow with the company. A few days later, you were called by a woman from the Personnel Department of MaryAnn's. She told you to come in to the main office for an interview with Mr. Allen. You are there now, five minutes early.

You and Mr. Allen

SECRETARY: What can I do for you?

YOU: _____

_____

SECRETARY: All right. Take this application and fill it out. (You fill out the application and wait. Finally the secretary calls you.)

SECRETARY: Mr. Allen will see you now.

YOU: _____

(You walk into Mr. Allen's office.)

MR. ALLEN: Hello. My name is Bernie Allen. Did you complete your application?

YOU: _____

MR. ALLEN: Let's have it. Take a seat.

YOU: _____

(Mr. Allen looks over your application.)

MR. ALLEN: What were your best subjects at school?

YOU: _____

_____

MR. ALLEN: Tell me about your work experience.

YOU: _____

_____

_____

_____

MR. ALLEN: Did you ever have any trouble on the job?

YOU: _____

_____

_____

MR. ALLEN: Our restaurants get real busy. How are you at handling pressure?

YOU: _____

_____

_____

MR. ALLEN: Well, then, let me tell you about the jobs we have open. The pay is four dollars and fifty cents ($4.50) an hour to start. You train for both counter work and cooking. There is a week of training on the day shift at one of our older restaurants. Then you start work on the day shift at the new restaurant. Later, you can be put on different shifts. It's a 40-hour week. The training will be at the MaryAnn's next to the car wash at Twenty-Third Avenue and Bank Road. Do you know where the new restaurant is?

YOU: _____

MR. ALLEN: It's on the corner of Third
Avenue and Main Street. What kind of
transportation would you be using?

YOU: _____

MR. ALLEN: Is there anything you want
to say about your health and physical
condition? You will need a health
certificate for the job.

YOU: _____

_____

MR. ALLEN: Working around money,
you would have to be bonded. Do you
know of any reason you couldn't be
bonded?

YOU: _____

_____

MR. ALLEN: Do you have any questions
about anything?

YOU: _____

_____

_____

MR. ALLEN: We have a little book about
that and many of the things we have
talked about. Here is a copy. It's called
Welcome to MaryAnn's Restaurants. Now
let me ask you something. Why would
you like to work for MaryAnn's?

YOU: _____

_____

_____

_____

_____

MR. ALLEN: And why do you think we
should hire you?

YOU: _____

_____

_____

_____

_____

MR. ALLEN: Well, I guess that covers
everything. Thank you for coming in. We
will be letting you know in about
a week.

YOU: _____

What Do You Think?

Rate Yourself

1. Read your test over carefully. Make any changes you want to make. Then rate yourself on each item below.

   Preparation
   ☐ Excellent   ☐ Fair
   ☐ Good   ☐ Poor

   Language
   ☐ Excellent   ☐ Fair
   ☐ Good   ☐ Poor

   Personality
   ☐ Excellent   ☐ Fair
   ☐ Good   ☐ Poor

   Attitude
   ☐ Excellent   ☐ Fair
   ☐ Good   ☐ Poor

   Motivation
   ☐ Excellent   ☐ Fair
   ☐ Good   ☐ Poor

   Qualifications
   ☐ Excellent   ☐ Fair
   ☐ Good   ☐ Poor

   Answering and Asking Questions
   ☐ Excellent   ☐ Fair
   ☐ Good   ☐ Poor

2. Do you think Mr. Allen would hire you?
   ☐ Yes   ☐ No   Why or why not?

   _____

   _____

   _____

   _____

3. What do you think you need to work on most before you go out for a real job interview?

   _____

   _____

   _____

   _____

4. How has this book helped you prepare to make a good impression on job interviewers?

   _____

   _____

   _____

Congratulations

on finishing the Janus Job Interview Guide!

Before you go out on real job interviews, review the Guidelines for Job Applicants on pages 8–15. And reread the interviews in which the applicants did the best job of presenting themselves. Good luck with your job search!